"TO HIM THAT BELIEVETH"

"TO HIM THAT ELIEVETH"

FREDERICK W. BABBEL

BOOKCRAFT • SALT LAKE CITY, UTAH

Library of Congress Catalog Card Number: 82-72513
ISBN O-88494-462-X

8th Printing, 1989

Lithographed in the United States of America
PUBLISHERS PRESS
Salt Lake City, Utah

Contents

A Word With You

"All things are possible to him that believeth." (Mark 9:23.) The challenges implied in *To Him That Believeth* may seem incredible to some. However, when you understand the principles involved and their implications with regard to your eternal destiny, you will realize that you really do determine your success in life or your lack of fulfillment!

Since writing *On Wings of Faith,* it has been my privilege to address and visit with hundreds of audiences all over the United States. Repeatedly people have expressed concern about how to activate the power of God in their lives. The eight subjects treated in this book deal with the needs most frequently expressed.

It has been disturbing to learn how few people have experienced the profound impact that these concepts have in shaping the more abundant life of which the Savior spoke.

There is more power available to you to determine your own successful course in life than you may have ever contemplated before. A few simple principles and keys embody the underlying solution to our problems. These principles are here, distilled from the scriptures and the wisdom of inspired leaders. Then they are applied to these major concerns in our lives. Incorporating these truths into your life will enable you to draw upon the very powers of heaven.

Whether you are young, in your prime, or in the sunset of life, none of the opportunities and resultant blessings outlined in this book are beyond your reach. You have the power to make today, and all the days that follow, a new life for yourself in spite of what may have happened in the past.

I challenge you to apply these principles in your life. With God's help you will succeed. Many lives have been profoundly elevated by them, and yours can be too.

— Frederick W. Babbel

Acknowledgments

I express my sincere gratitude to the numerous people, including officiators, staff members, visitors, and patrons of the Washington Temple, who have offered meaningful suggestions and continued encouragement in the writing of this book.

I also thank choice friends and associates who read and reviewed my writing. Special assistance was given to me by my dear friend Dr. Brendan Stack, who made available to my wife and myself the use of his cabin wherein much of this manuscript was prepared.

In all my efforts I have enjoyed the complete support, encouragement, and assistance of Marvin W. Wallin, George Bickerstaff, Ann St. Clair, and other staff members at Bookcraft, and I here express appreciation to them.

I give special thanks to my devoted wife, June, whose constant assistance and valued partnership have contributed much to this book. We have found our own lives profoundly stimulated by the spirit and message of this book.

*Because faith is wanting, the fruits
are. No man since the world was had
faith without having something along
with it . . . A man who has none of the
gifts has no faith; and he deceives
himself if he supposes he has.*
(Joseph Smith, *History of the Church* 5:218.
Hereinafter referred to as *DHC*.)

Building Powerful Faith

I learned a valuable lesson a number of years ago when my
wife and I visited the Grand Canyon in Arizona. We were at
the north rim when the naturalist guide showed us a twisted,
gnarled, old juniper tree which was literally growing out of the
side of the rock canyon wall by the lookout point. We wondered
how it could possibly continue to grow. Then our guide told us
an interesting bit of history in connection with this tree.

A juniper seed is shaped somewhat like a cantaloupe seed.
One of these little seeds fell into a crevice near the edge of the
canyon wall. Everything was solid rock. It appeared that the
seed could not possibly germinate since there was no soil, little if
any water, and virtually no sunshine down in this crevice. Yet
this little seed was not concerned about these limits. It had but
one burning desire and that was to fulfill the measure of its
creation!

In a manner that we cannot fathom, that little seed germinated, implanted roots into that solid rock, and began to grow. Gradually it raised a shoot through the crevice where it could seek sunshine and a little rain.

As it continued to grow and expand into a full-fledged, though misshapen, tree, its trunk and its roots began to exert a continuing pressure on the outer ledge of rock. Finally the pressure became so great that one entire large section of the canyon wall broke loose and crumbled into a massive heap near the base of the canyon, nearly one mile straight down.

The guide said it was estimated that forty million tons of rock lay at the base of this tremendous canyon because that little seed didn't know it could not grow. It just wouldn't give up.

No one is beaten until he stops trying. No one!

Essential Components of Faith

How often we have heard the admonition, ". . . without faith no man pleaseth God. . . ." (D&C 63:11.) We need to discover how to grow in faith. We also need experience. A living faith is a priceless possession and the quest for it is worthy of our combined energies of mind, body, and spirit.

Persistence is one of the essential components of faith. Don't give up! "That which we persist in doing becomes easier to do; not that the nature of the thing itself has changed, but that our power to do is increased!" (Heber J. Grant, *Gospel Standards*, comp. G. Homer Durham [Salt Lake City: Improvement Era, 1944], p. 355.)

Acting "as if" is another one.

> Begin thinking of faith in terms of "something to do" rather than something to "have."
>
> Faith must not be of the kind that sits and holds its hands, but rather the sort of faith that spurs one on to work tirelessly and relentlessly.
>
> If it makes a man work — and keep on working — it is genuine.
>
> You must act as if you knew your success were already assured or you'll never make the necessary efforts. . . . There is nothing mysterious about it. You don't even have to "feel" faith. If you'll only begin to act "as if," then the feeling . . . will come of its own

accord. (Elmer Wheeler, *The Wealth Within You* [New York City, Prentice-Hall, 1955], pp. 62. Hereinafter referred to as *The Wealth Within You.*)

Faith and works go together. It is impossible to have faith without accompanying work or action.

> Faith is not a substitute for work. It is not a substitute for preparation. Rather it is a necessary part of these things. There is nothing which can be demonstrated and pointed to as faith except in relation to work. The man who says he has faith he can do something and then does nothing, has never known faith for it comes into being only at the point of action. If he had had faith he would have done something. . . . Faith is an expressed affirmative attitude. (*The Wealth Within You*, p. 65.)

Note that these three factors apply to achieving anything in life: fame, fortune, and material possessions. They are also essential for building spiritual strength.

A different kind of work or action may be required to achieve a spiritual goal. Your "work" might consist of prayer or continuing gratitude. Or it might be being sufficiently "in tune" to be able to learn God's will and follow his direction. (If you have faith enough in yourself to move a mountain, get a shovel. If you have faith enough in the Lord to move a mountain, get out of the way!)

We must remember that eternal blessings come only when we are in harmony with the powers of heaven and draw upon them. How to achieve such harmony will be discussed in subsequent chapters.

When we manifest faith in the Lord Jesus Christ, we put those forces in motion that will open the doors to the blessings of heaven. For instance, "Behold, I say unto you that whoso believeth in Christ, doubting nothing, whatsoever he shall ask the Father in the name of Christ it shall be granted him; And this promise is unto all, even unto the ends of the earth." (Mormon 9:21; see also verses 25, 28.)

This establishes the fact that it is an eternal law that he who comes to God, doubting nothing, shall have whatsoever he asks. Exercising great and mighty faith will set divine energy into action by the mind or will.

Fruits of Great Faith

The fruits of great faith in human lives can be illustrated by a number of cases with which I am personally familiar.

The first series concerns Fritz Lehnig, one of our faithful district presidents in Germany when I was there on my first mission. Some of the missionaries used to refer to him as "the Moses of the mission." My first acquaintance with him began when President Heber J. Grant was touring the European missions in 1937.

Be Quiet While the Prophet Speaks

A large congregation of approximately fifteen hundred Saints and investigators was gathered in the city of Breslau, Germany (now Wroclaw, Poland) to hear the prophet. Several district presidents from that general area were on the stand along with the mission president and special guests.

As President Grant arose to address the congregation, a small child near the front of the hall began creating quite a disturbance. Without a word, Brother Lehnig left his seat on the stand, walked down to this little child and placed his hands upon this child's head, commanding it, in the name of Jesus Christ, to be quiet while the prophet spoke. From that moment on there was no further disturbance. Such was this good man's simple faith.

Send Brother Fritz Lehnig Twenty Marks

A short time later, one of our branch presidents, Brother Woolf, in the city of Weimar, was working on his branch books at home. All at once, he heard a voice distinctly say to him, "Send Brother Fritz Lehnig twenty marks!"

He was startled and puzzled and thought, "Why should such a request come to me? I have never heard of Fritz Lehnig. Who is he?"

He concluded that perhaps someone was trying to play a practical joke on him and asked his wife in the nearby kitchen, "Did you just say something to me?" She assured him that this was not the case. Then he asked her if any of the children were still at home. Again the answer was negative. Brother Woolf decided that he was probably mistaken in thinking that someone had spoken to him, and returned to his work.

He had barely resumed his task when he heard again, in a more insistent voice, "Send Brother Fritz Lehnig twenty marks!" This time he jumped to his feet and hurried out of the house to look around. Not finding anyone, he again asked his wife the same questions as before and again she reassured him that she had said nothing.

Upon returning to his room, he decided to check the register of Church leadership in the other German-speaking missions. There he learned that Brother Lehnig was the district president of the Spreewald District of the East German Mission. His address was included. Brother Woolf then decided to follow a hunch and send him ten marks. As he was reaching for the money in his small cash box, an imperative voice said again, "Send Brother Lehnig *twenty* marks!"

Without further hesitation he addressed an envelope, inserted the twenty marks, and penciled a hasty note saying, in effect, "Dear Brother Lehnig: I don't know you from Adam. Will you please write and tell me why I am sending you twenty marks?"

These two men met each other for the first time a few days later when President J. Reuben Clark came to Berlin on a special assignment by the President of the United States. During his stay he arranged to speak to the Saints who could conveniently come to Berlin. After an inspirational message, he requested that the remaining time be turned over to members in the congregation for testimony bearing.

The first person to rise to his feet was Brother Fritz Lehnig. He related how he had been on the verge of losing his home. A seven-year mortgage was due with the entire principal and interest. After contacting every possible source to obtain the necessary amount, he found that he was still twenty marks short and the debt was due the following day.

In simple faith he prayed to the Lord. He reminded him of the problem and what he had done to handle it. He concluded by asking the Lord to do his part since he needed the remaining twenty marks by the next morning to avoid losing his home.

Then he explained how he had received Brother Woolf's letter with the necessary amount and expressed thanks for this blessing.

Brother Woolf, who was also in the audience, wasted no time in hurrying over to embrace Brother Lehnig and then told his side of the episode. What a beautiful testimonial of the power of a living faith!

Faith Overcomes Cancer

A few weeks later, Fritz Lehnig's son, Reinhold, went to the Berlin mission home to deliver a beautiful hand-fashioned replica of the Ulm cathedral, the tallest spired cathedral in Germany. It was sent as a farewell gift for President Kelly, mission president, who was leaving soon to return home.

President Kelly, being a physician and surgeon, inquired of Reinhold as to his mother's present condition. He was aware that she was struggling with terminal cancer. Reinhold reported that the doctor had sent his mother home to die, feeling that she had only a few more days to live.

"President Kelly, we are not discouraged. Dad and I are fasting. On Sunday, Dad is giving Mother a blessing to be healed of this cancer. With this blessing he will also make a covenant with the Lord to send me on a mission when she is healed."

About two weeks later Brother Fritz Lehnig advised President Kelly by telephone that Reinhold was ready to report for his mission. Sister Lehnig had been completely healed of her cancer.

The Crushed Hand and Wrist

I felt that this would probably be the last experience I would hear concerning Brother Lehnig's faith, since I was being transferred to another mission. A few years later, however, I found myself back in Germany with Elder Ezra Taft Benson, right after World War II had ended. On this occasion Elder Benson had invited all of the district presidents in the East German Mission to meet with him in Berlin.

Three of our brethren, one of whom was Brother Lehnig, were boarding a freight train near the Polish border. After the war ended, virtually no passenger cars remained, and people had to board dilapidated freight or cattle cars to reach their destination by rail. They would crowd into these boxcars like so many sheep. When the boxcars were filled inside, the people would hang on to the outside or climb and ride on the top.

As these three men sought space, they found it necessary to climb to the top of one of these boxcars. Apparently this space was already overcrowded, and one of their number was shoved off. As he fell to the station platform and lay sprawled, a large truck, running on its rims (tires were not available), ran over his hand and wrist, badly mangling them.

In this painful condition he called for help. His two companions climbed down and picked him up to take him to the nearest first-aid station. As they did so, this wounded brother pleaded, "Brethren, I have come here to go with you to our meeting in Berlin. I want you to bless me so that I can be there, too."

His companions laid their hands upon his head. Brother Lehnig pronounced the blessing. As they took their hands from his head, they saw that his hand and wrist had been restored and were as whole as they had been before the accident.

Rejoicing, they arrived a few hours later at the appointed meeting. They related this incident to those present and we could see no signs even of bruises on the hand and wrist. That simple faith had again moved the powers of heaven.

We Have a Date With the Lord

More recently, I met in the Washington Temple one of my missionary associates from my first mission. He related to me an unforgettable experience.

He and his companion had been scheduled to hold a street meeting one afternoon. But since rain was pouring down in torrents, they informed President Lehnig that the street meeting would have to be cancelled because no one would be willing to stop and listen in such driving rain. Brother Lehnig responded: "Brethren, we have a date with the Lord. Put on your raincoats, get your umbrellas, and we'll be on our way."

Two reluctant elders followed his counsel. When they arrived at their selected site, people were scurrying in all directions to get out of the rain. Many were huddled in doorways, waiting for the rain to abate.

With the rain pouring down, one of the elders offered an opening prayer. As they opened their eyes, they were met with a strange sight. They witnessed the rain streaming down, but a strange semicircular area around them was completely free of rain. The steady downpour looked much like a theater curtain protecting them.

People huddled in the doorways and others hurrying to get out of the rain noticed this strange phenomenon and crowded into this rain-free section. The elders had a virtually captive audience to listen to them that afternoon. They had kept their date with the Lord.

The Age of Miracles Is Not Past

Quite recently I was invited to speak at a meeting for all the Church leadership in Wisconsin. When I arrived in Milwaukee, I was greeted by a representative from Salt Lake City and by the Regional Representative serving this area. I inquired how we should share the time at this Friday evening meeting and was informed that they wished me to take the entire time.

In the process of my remarks at the meeting, I related some of the faith-promoting stories that have been included in this section of the book. The Regional Representative walked to the lectern after I finished and announced, "Brothers and sisters, I told Brother Babbel that I did not wish to speak this evening, but I must."

He then related how he, as a citizen of East Germany, had met Elder Benson and myself in Berlin right after the war and how he had volunteered for missionary service. He bore witness of the things I had related, as he was personally acquainted with Brother Lehnig and the extraordinary events of this man's life. He also spoke of his own escape from East Germany and his subsequent United States citizenship. Then he continued:

"Brothers and Sisters, I have just returned from East Germany where the Brethren in Salt Lake sent me to meet with our

Church leadership. We held our meetings successfully in East Berlin.

"As I was preparing to return to my hotel in West Berlin, I suddenly realized that I had left my American passport and all of my identification materials in my hotel room. Without such documentation I would not be permitted to leave East Berlin, particularly since I had escaped years earlier and would be regarded as an escapee, to probably be imprisoned and tried in an East German court. This really concerned me and filled me with fear.

"This Brother Lehnig, about whom Brother Babbel spoke, was walking with me along the street which leads to the Brandenburger Tor, the large memorial arch that separates East and West Berlin. When I told him of my dilemma, he put his arm on my shoulder and said, 'Brother Walter, I want you to remember one thing. The age of miracles is not past! Now I want you to do exactly what I tell you to do. I want you to walk down the middle of the street under the arch. Do not look to the right or the left. Do not stop to ask or answer any questions. Just keep walking straight ahead until you reach the safety of West Berlin.'

"Being well acquainted with Brother Lehnig's faith, I decided to do as he directed, but I confess that inwardly I was trembling. I began walking toward the arch. Four military police, armed with automatic weapons, were standing on each side as I passed under the arch. When I was opposite them I continued to walk and expected momentarily to feel bullets in my back. All at once I realized that I was past the archway and standing in the free territory of West Berlin!

"As I turned around to look, I could see Brother Lehnig waving and seeming to say to me, 'See, Brother Walter, the age of miracles is not past!' "

He concluded his message with this stirring testimony: "Brothers and Sisters, I stand before you alive today because of the faith of that man. Either the Lord cloaked me in invisibility so I could go past those guards, or else he blinded their eyes so they could not see me. I am with you today because of that man's faith."

Healed by a Prayer of Faith

While I was serving as Secretary of the Melchizedek Priesthood Committee of the Church, my office was situated next to that of Elder Henry D. Moyle. One morning he asked me to step into his office.

"Do you happen to know the young man who wrote me this letter?" he asked as he handed me the letter.

I recognized the name of a young German brother whom I had met, first on my first mission and again in Berlin after the end of World War II.

As a baby, just a few months old, this young man had been left unattended momentarily on a kitchen table. He rolled off and injured his body so severely that one side of his body became paralyzed and a large hump formed on his back. When I first saw him, his pathetic appearance as a deformed cripple filled me with great sympathy. Elder Moyle confided that he had shared similar feelings years earlier when he became acquainted with this young man while he, Elder Moyle, was serving a mission there.

This young man was now serving as a missionary and described a recent happening. His mission president had asked him to visit several nearby large cities in an effort to locate some of the refugee Saints so that the Church welfare program and Church activity might again become a part of their shattered lives.

As he prepared to leave, his body was covered with large sores and wherever his metal body brace rubbed against them, they began to bleed. Not only was this extremely painful, but also his clothing became so blood-soaked that it was impossible for him to continue.

In desperation, he removed his metal braces, his tenth set since he was a young child. Without them he was totally incapable of moving from place to place.

Then he explained how he had fallen to his knees at his bedside and pleaded with the Lord to heal him so he might fulfill this special assignment.

His faith was not in vain. For the first time in his life he was able to stand erect, with his paralysis gone, the hump removed from his shoulders, and the sores removed from his body. His faith had made him whole! And then, after this happened, he expressed his gratitude for having been blessed to accomplish the assignment given him.

As Elder Moyle and I finished reading this moving letter, our eyes were filled with tears and our hearts were overflowing with gratitude for the Lord's blessings to this humble missionary. God forgets not his own.

Foundation for Abundant Family Living

Ear Infection Healed

When Elder Ezra Taft Benson was selected by President Eisenhower to serve as Secretary of Agriculture, I was asked to work as an Assistant to the Secretary. Three weeks after our family moved to Washington, D.C., and our children came down with chicken pox, our fourth child was born.

At this time our oldest daughter contracted a severe ear infection. The pediatrician gave her an injection and advised irrigating the ear frequently to flush out the infection. He also prescribed nose drops, ear drops, and medication by mouth every four hours. With a new baby, this made our schedule rather hectic.

Several days later our second daughter became ill with a high fever and complained of aching ears. The doctor said it looked like the same thing, only worse, and prescribed the same treatment.

A short time later, our second daughter was lying on the front room couch. We had just completed a prayer at her side when we heard a knock at the door. What a joy it was to find Secretary Benson coming to visit us and have a look at the new baby!

We proudly showed him our new baby girl. As we were visiting, our daughter on the couch, who was just four years old at the time, spoke up. "Daddy, could you and Brother Benson give me a blessing so that I will be well?"

We knelt at the side of the couch and gave her a blessing. Within an hour the fever broke, and there was no further trouble.

My wife describes what happened after I left with Brother Benson.

"I had not been able to hear the blessing, and when they had finished, I pulled my husband aside and asked him if she was to be healed, if the infection had been rebuked. He assured me that she would be well and not to worry about it. Our daughter still was very hot and very still. As time passed, I wondered if I should give her some of the medication we had bought on the way home. After all, it was already paid for. I knew she would be healed. There was no question of that, but we had the medicine on hand and might as well use it. At least it wouldn't hurt her. Then I realized, *The Lord doesn't need any medicine, and he is healing her.* As soon as I decided this, her fever dropped dramatically. Before that, even after the blessing, there had been no change. It seemed to me that I had to make up my mind to depend wholly upon the Lord before she could be healed."

That night I could hear our oldest daughter crying. When I reached her bed she pleaded, "Daddy, my ear is really hurting. Won't you give me a blessing like you gave Julene so I'll be all right?" In the quiet of that night I fulfilled her request and she was healed.

Under normal circumstances we had always made it a practice to administer to our children when sickness was present. Why did we not administer to our children in the first place? We did not even think of it. Either the moving, the chicken pox, work, and the new baby weighed us down, or our forgetfulness was meant to make the experience an object lesson in faith — which it was!

You Have to Be Healed by Tomorrow Morning

At Brigham Young University our daughter, Julene, helped organize a singing group of about fifty students. They called themselves the "Y Americans." Their purpose was to sing patriotic songs and get Americans to appreciate their heritage. Many of these songs were written or arranged by Julene, and she was also their accompanist.

One Friday morning she called to announce that Ed Sullivan had invited this group to appear on his nationwide television show in New York City. She mentioned that the group was to meet for a special videotaping session on the following day, and that the tape was to be sent to New York.

That afternoon her older sister, Bonnie, called to tell us that Julene in her excitement had tripped and fallen down the stairs. She had chipped the bone in her left thumb, ripped the nail, and developed a paralysis in her left arm, apparently from a pinched nerve. The doctor had told her that it would be weeks before she could use her arm again, provided that the paralysis left.

Julene was filled with pain and disappointment. My wife suggested that she would have to get someone to take her place.

"But Mother," came the reply, "that isn't possible. No one can play this music but me."

"Surely someone on campus could learn it."

"It isn't written down. I made the arrangements and played them by ear. There is no way it could be written in time for tomorrow's taping."

"Then they'll have to cancel the taping."

"That's impossible. It takes a couple of weeks to set one up and get all of the people together."

Her mother continues: "I thought there was no way — save a miracle — that would make it possible for the scheduled videotaping to take place. Thoughts quickly flitted through my mind. The Ed Sullivan show was a worldly thing, not necessarily the sort of thing that would justify asking such a favor of the Lord. But was there anything wrong with asking for help? I finally convinced myself it was all right. There was no other way I could see that she could make it, short of asking for a miracle.

"About 5:00 P.M., Provo time, she called again. The numbness was wearing off and Julene was in great pain. The dispensary was closed for the weekend. The doctors had gone home, and the girls did not know how to contact them. They had not prescribed any painkillers because the paralysis had made them wary of doing so.

"I said, 'Without a miracle there's no way you can play tomorrow. Is there anyone in the city of Provo who would have courage enough to give you such a blessing?' The girls could not think of anyone.

"I remembered that there would be a family reunion in Salt Lake City that evening, and told her to do four specific things:

"First, take a couple of aspirins to help ease your pain as you travel to Salt Lake City to the family reunion.

"Then, have Bonnie take you to the reunion and find someone there who is willing to give you the blessing you need. Specify that you need them to bless you so you can play tomorrow morning. Don't just ask for a blessing. Be specific.

"Now, when it hurts, don't dwell on how much it hurts, but immediately talk to your Heavenly Father. Tell him how grateful you are that he loves you and that he knows what to do to help your hand.

"Finally, every time you think about it, visualize yourself as if you were watching a movie about how you will look tomorrow. Think of your pink dress. Your hair. Then see yourself starting the rehearsal, sitting down at the piano, and starting to play the octaves with your left hand. Then lift your hands up, look at them, grin, and say, 'It worked! I can play!' and start playing again. You must see yourself this way over and over again. If you wake up during the night, put that 'movie' back into your mind as often as you need to. We'll fast and pray until we hear from you tomorrow after the taping program. And then, next week, we'll come to New York to see the show with you.

"Our entire family was instructed to do the same thing. We fasted. We prayed. We expressed our gratitude and we visualized her being able to play."

The following day in the late afternoon we received a call from an excited, happy girl. "Dad," came her voice, "I was healed! It was just like we visualized it! When I got up Saturday morning, my arm was really hurting and I still couldn't move my thumb. But I wasn't worried. I visualized my arm to be well again and got ready. While the group warmed up, I didn't play for them. I just sat at the piano with my arm in the sling. But when the actual taping began, the paralysis was gone, and I could play. I played for seven hours until we finished the taping. I'll see you in New York on Thursday."

The next day my wife's mother called from Ogden, Utah. She was crying. "It was a miracle!" she said. "If you could only have seen her Friday night; I've never seen anything like it!" Then she held the receiver away so we could hear Julene banging away on the piano for her cousins.

What a tremendous thrill it was for us and for Julene to realize that the power of her faith had been manifested to that extent!

That weekend in New York we witnessed a beautiful performance.

Dislocated Knee Healed Overnight

About two weeks later Julene called up and said, "Dad, this time I've really blown it. Last night after a dance we were all piling into the car when my knee hit the door frame and I dislocated it. The doctor has put me in a flexible cast. It will probably be eight weeks before the cast can be removed, so I won't be able to come home with Bonnie for the summer as we had planned."

I replied, "Julene, have you so soon forgotten the lesson you just learned in connection with the Ed Sullivan show?" There was a long silence.

"I get the message, Dad," came the reply.

The following morning Julene called us again. "Dad, I've taken off the cast. I'll be home with Bonnie as we had planned!"

Faith Cures Headache Almost Instantly

As we were coming home from a speaking assignment a few weeks later, Julene asked her mother if she had an aspirin. "My head is just splitting and every little jiggle on the road makes it worse."

Then I reminded her, "Julene, have you so soon forgotten the lessons you learned recently?"

She replied, "Do you think it will work on a headache, too?"

"Why not?" was my answer.

Without another word she turned around and, looking straight ahead, said a silent prayer. In a minute or two she turned back, grinned, and said, "Well, Dad, it's gone!"

When the Shoe Is on the Other Foot

In July I was responsible for the annual Stake Summeree for our Explorer Scouts and Mia Maids. I was loading the car alone at a friend's house, placing in the trunk of the car two very large and heavy cooking grills covered with grease. I had managed to get the first one loaded without incident. As I was putting the second one in, it began to slip out of one hand. I instinctively reached forward to get another grip. In doing so I threw out my lower back. With great difficulty I dragged myself into the car and drove home. Once there, as I opened the car door, I literally tumbled out onto the driveway. My children picked me up and helped me into the house.

I was lying on the front hall floor in intense pain when my daughter, Julene, came up and said, "Well, Dad, what are you going to do about it?"

Gritting my teeth with pain, I replied, "You're really putting me on the spot, aren't you?"

She grinned and said, "I intend to do just that!"

After a few moments I knew what I had to do. I answered, "Since you put it to me that way, I'm going to get up in a few minutes and take a hot soaking tub bath. Then I'm going outdoors and take a long walk to get myself in condition. Tomorrow morning I'm going to go to church and climb upstairs where I will be teaching our high priests group. How do you like that?"

"That's fine, Dad," came the response.

Well, that's exactly what I had to do. And I did it! But I had to manifest that power of faith which I had tried to instill in my children. I had to draw upon the powers of heaven myself.

Powerful Faith Confirmed

These and many other experiences have been related to verify that through a living faith, we may draw upon the powers of heaven. Here it seems appropriate to consider the Lord's promise in the Doctrine and Covenants.

> . . . he that hath faith in me to be healed, and is not appointed unto death, shall be healed.
>
> He who hath faith to see shall see.
>
> He who hath faith to hear shall hear.
>
> The lame who hath faith to leap shall leap. (D&C 42:48-51.)

Elder Orson F. Whitney dealt with this "mainspring of power" and shared with us one challenging thought:

> God deals with men according to their faith. The Savior wrought mighty miracles by his own faith, but most of them were where faith abounded in the hearts of the people. In other places he did not do many mighty works "because of their unbelief." Faith is a gift from God, and they who serve him best have most of it. Faith is the soil that brings forth miracles. "All things are possible to them that believe." (*Saturday Night Thoughts* [Salt Lake City: Deseret News, 1921], p. 283.)

Should we not always say, "not as I will, but as thou wilt"? (Matthew 26:39.)

The will of God is quite clear. God ministers on earth to bless, not to curse or afflict us. "I am come that they might have life, and that they might have it more abundantly" (John 10:10) was the Savior's clarion call. His challenge to us was to "Be ye therefore perfect, even as your Father which is in heaven is perfect." (Matthew 5:48.) If Christ wants us to be perfect, is not that the mind and will of God? Let us cease seeking to justify our doubts, fears, faintings, weaknesses, and anxieties. These are not of God. We are seldom justified in trying to rationalize our negative thoughts when we consider the scripture, "Not my will but thine be done."

One of Elder James E. Talmage's radio talks entitled "O Ye of Little Faith" offers us some practical counsel:

> Faith includes a moving, vital, inspiring confidence in God, and the acceptance of His will as our law and of His words as our guide in life. Faith in God is a principle of power, for by its exercise spiritual forces are made operative; and by this power phenomena that appear to be super-natural, such as we call miracles, are wrought.
> . . .

It is beyond question that faith in the Lord Jesus Christ as the Savior and Redeemer is essential to salvation. But this kind of faith is possible to him only who seeks it in earnestness and is receptive to its influences; for, be it known that faith is a gift from God. (See Eph. 2:8.) The gift is free to all who desire it. Ask for it, strive for it, and it shall be given you! Seek it, and you shall not fail to find! Proof that you have received will be manifest in what you do with it. (*Sunday Night Talks by Radio* [Salt Lake City, The Church of Jesus Christ of Latter-day Saints, 1931], pp. 121, 125. Hereinafter referred to as *Sunday Night Talks.*)

We need to kindle a powerful faith. We need to manifest a living faith. We need to accept the things that we ask of God as being fulfilled. If a person asks his father for bread, will he give him a stone? If we, as mortals, are able to give good gifts to those who ask, how much greater is the love which moves God to fulfill his divine promise! "What things soever ye desire, when ye pray, believe that ye receive them, and ye shall have them." (Mark 11:24.)

This is the will of God. Let it be made manifest in you. For miracles have not ceased, neither should they cease. When they cease, it is because we have rationalized and placed ourselves out of the reach of those powers by which these wonderful gifts may be made manifest.

As the Prophet Joseph Smith explained, we may feel that we have certain divine gifts. If the fruits of those gifts are lacking, we deceive ourselves. Gifts come and remain with us through faith. When faith is lacking, so are the gifts and the fruits of those gifts.

The prophet Moroni gives us a fitting challenge and wise counsel near the end of his record.

Wherefore, my beloved brethren, have miracles ceased because Christ hath ascended into heaven . . .

And because he hath done this, my beloved brethren, have miracles ceased? Behold, I say unto you, Nay; neither have angels ceased to minister unto the children of men.

For behold, they are subject unto him, to minister according to the word of his command, showing themselves unto them of strong faith and a firm mind in every form of godliness. . . .

Or have angels ceased to appear unto the children of men? Or has he withheld the power of the Holy Ghost from them? Or will he, so long as time shall last, or the earth shall stand, or there shall be one man upon the face thereof to be saved?

Behold, I say unto you, Nay; for it is by faith that miracles are wrought; and it is by faith that angels appear and minister unto men; wherefore, if these things have ceased wo be unto the children of men, for it is because of unbelief, and all is vain. (Moroni 7:27, 29-30, 36-37.)

Remember, with faith, all things are possible. That is why we must be actively engaged in building a powerful faith. In this we must not fail.

What have we learned so far about developing a powerful faith?

1. Be persistent.
2. Act "as if."
3. Work for it.
4. Doubt nothing.
5. Faith is a gift of God.

Let this mind be in you, which was
also in Christ Jesus,

Who, being in the form of God, thought it not
robbery to be equal with God.
(Philippians 2:5-6.)

A son of God, like God to be,
Would not be robbing Deity;
And he who has this hope within,
Will purify himself from sin.
(Lorenzo Snow, *Improvement Era,* June 1919, 22:660.)

Shaping Your Destiny

God works according to eternal principles. His help is available to all who have need and desire and trust, regardless of church affiliation. Sometimes a person will have an experience that will completely change his perspective about life. My former business partner is a good example.

In 1920 he experienced his death while lying on the operating table. The doctor had promised to attempt to remove a large tumor from his jugular vein. My partner witnessed the entire operation as his spirit hovered over his body, and he overheard the conversation between the doctor and nurse. At one point, the doctor said, "I can't go on. If I do, he will die."

"But you promised him you would make the effort," said the nurse, "even if it should cost his life. You must keep your promise."

During the operation, as the doctor had feared, the jugular vein split open and blood began to gush from the wound.

My partner's spirit left the room at this point, and he found himself entering into the spirit world where he net loved ones who had departed earlier. All at once he was env·'loped in a brilliant white light.

"I have brought you back into my presence," said the voice in the midst of the dazzling white light, "because you have so greatly feared the transition which you call death. You now perceive that there is nothing to fear, but rather the opportunity to enjoy a boundless future much more glorious than that which you have known."

Then this glorious personage continued: "You must return to the earth. Your mission in life is not yet finished. You will lose all that you have held dear and cherished. However, if you will trust me, you shall yet accomplish many great things and realize some of the sweetest blessings that are available for my Father's children upon the earth."

Upon returning to his body, which was now covered with a sheet, he saw the nurse preparing to leave the room. As his spirit reentered his body, the nurse noticed movement and breathing. She called out excitedly, "Doctor! Come back! He's alive and breathing again!" Then my partner lapsed into unconsciousness.

As he left the hospital, the Mother Superior said to him, "We never expected you to leave here alive. You were dead for several minutes!"

All that he had been told during his brief interview in the spirit world happened. He did lose virtually everything that he had held dear, including his wife who divorced him and claimed his earthly possessions. Shortly before the infamous events at Pearl Harbor in 1941, he became a member of The Church of Jesus Christ of Latter-day Saints and soon thereafter married a beautiful returned lady missionary. Bounteous blessings continue to be enjoyed by that couple and their family.

Most of us do not have such a dramatic experience to force us to evaluate and take charge of our lives. Yet whether we are aware of it or not, knowingly or unknowingly, we do shape our own destiny. Our challenge is to learn the principles that will help us. But first we must know the answer to the question, "Who am I?"

You Are Somebody!

You are not a nobody. You are a *somebody*—a real somebody with unlimited potential!

"Who, me?" you may reply. Yes, you. You are literally a son or daughter of God. He is the actual father of the divine spirit that dwells within your mortal body and gives it life. When that spirit leaves your body, you are pronounced dead.

Even more significant, being an offspring of deity—God—is the very reason that once in the Old Testament, and again in the New Testament, God declared, "Ye are gods." (Psalm 82:6; John 10:34.)

You are of the family of our Heavenly Father. And you are endowed with the potential, if you choose to use it, of becoming like your divine Father.

"That seems incredible!" you may exclaim. "Do we have any valid proof that this is really the case?"

"Genuine and inspiring proof," comes the response, "through prophets from our day as well as from sacred records we call scripture. This is part of your legacy from God."

Perhaps the best-known expression relevant to this subject was penned by President Lorenzo Snow in 1840: "As man now is, God once was: As God now is, man may be." (*Biography and Family Records of Lorenzo Snow* [Salt Lake City: Zion's Book Store, 1975], p. 46.)

We will consider three inspired declarations to confirm and amplify the statements already made.

In his memorable King Follett Sermon, the Prophet Joseph Smith identified clearly the genesis of man:

> The soul—the mind of man—the immortal spirit—where did it come from? All learned men and doctors of divinity say that God created it in the beginning; but it is not so: the very idea lessens man in my estimation. I do not believe the doctrine. I know better.
>
> Hear it, all ye ends of the world, for God has told me so. If you don't believe me, it will not make the truth without effect. . . .

We say that God himself is a self-existent being. Who told you so? It is correct enough, but how did it get into your heads? Who told you that man did not exist in like manner upon the same principles? Man does exist upon the same principles. . . . The mind or the intelligence which man possesses is co-equal [co-eternal] with God himself! I know my testimony is true. The intelligence of spirits had no beginning, neither will it have an end. . . . The first principles of man are self-existent with God. (*DHC* 6:310.)

What about man's next phase of existence? How did he become an offspring of deity? Parley P. Pratt clarified this issue:

This individual, spiritual body was begotten by the Heavenly Father, in his own likeness and image, and by the laws of procreation. It was born and matured in the heavenly mansions, trained in the school of love in the family circle, and amid the most tender embraces of parental and fraternal affection. In this primeval probation, in its heavenly home, it lived and moved as a free and rational intelligence, acting upon its own agency, and like all intelligence, independent in its own sphere.

It was placed under certain laws and was responsible to its Patriarchal Head. (*Key to the Science of Theology* [Salt Lake City: Deseret Book Co., 1938], p. 56. Hereinafter referred to as *Key to Theology.*)

Let us now bring our present and future state of existence into proper focus. For this information we turn to Elder James E. Talmage:

Man as an individual is eternal, for he is literally the child of the eternal father of spirits, veritably born in the lineage of the Gods!

Before birth, now and after death, each of us has been, is, and shall be a distinct personage — the same being throughout, of unchanging identity and therefore everlasting.

You were you and I was I before we were born into these bodies of flesh. You shall be yourself and I shall be myself beyond the grave. This body of ours is the earth-garment of the immortal spirit. . . .

There is in man an immortal spirit that lived as an intelligent being before the body was formed, and that shall continue to exist as the same immortal individual after the body has gone to decay. . . .

Divine revelation attests that gloriously surpassing truth, man is of eternal nature. (*Sunday Night Talks,* no. 21, p. 230.)

There you have it. Through these inspired declarations, we begin to realize who we are and what we may become. The answer to the admonition of Socrates, "Man, know thyself," is thus unfolded.

You, the Maker of Your Destiny

Each one of us is now in the process of becoming the kind of person we must live with throughout eternity. Yet relatively few of us realize the unlimited potential we possess as literal sons and daughters of our Great Father and God. Fewer yet have discovered how to communicate actively with the powers of heaven. And only an insignificant number have realized in their lives the invitation and the promise of Jesus Christ when he said:

> Behold, I stand at the door, and knock: If any man hear my voice, and open the door, I will come in to him, and will sup with him, and he with me.
> To him that overcometh will I grant to sit with me in my throne, even as I also overcame, and am set down with my Father in his throne. (Revelation 3:20-21.)

That is what this book is all about—to clarify the challenges to be met and to outline the foundation, the building blocks that will enable all who will apply themselves to enjoy a life of greater power and purpose than most of us have dreamed possible.

Whether you are young, in your prime, or in the sunset of life, none of the opportunities outlined in this book are beyond your reach. You have the power to make today, and all the days that follow, what you will, in spite of what has happened in the past.

While the scriptures affirm that Jesus Christ is the author and the finisher of our faith, the very suggestion that you are the author and the finisher of your destiny may seem startling. However, when you understand the principles involved and their implications with regard to your eternal destiny, you will perceive that it is you who determines your success in life or your lack of fulfillment. There is more power available to you to shape your destiny—your own successful course in life—than you ever contemplated before. Abiding by these principles will make the very powers of heaven available for your benefit.

Eternal Principles of Progression

In this chapter we will examine two principles and two keys through which we may increase our faith and apply it in shaping our destiny.

Law of the Harvest

The first principle is the Law of the Harvest.

> . . . whatsoever a man soweth, that shall he also reap. (Galatians 6:7.)

Some people call this the Law of Cause and Effect; others call it the Law of Action and Reaction; still others call it the Law of Karma. References in the holy scriptures usually refer to it as the Law of the Harvest. This law can be named as the first law given during the creation of this earth and all forms of life thereon. (See Genesis 1:11-12, 27-28.)

Everything multiplies "after his kind." This includes plants, fruit trees, birds, fish, insects, animals, and human beings. If you plant a carrot seed, you won't get a tomato. If you want a tomato, you will have to plant the right kind of seed.

A seed does not just return one seed and does not remain just a planted seed. If you plant a watermelon seed and nourish it, it will grow into a melon vine with several watermelons, each containing hundreds of seeds. Likewise, a kernel of corn does not return just a single kernel of corn. And the conception of a child results in a future father or mother, a grandfather or grandmother.

As we apply this principle to daily life situations, we will discern that it also applies to our thoughts, feelings, and actions.

In one of the training courses which I directed at the National Archives, we had several personnel attending from the Navy's David Taylor Model Basin near Washington, D.C. Since we were considering the principles and practices of good management, I discussed these concepts with them as they applied to their specific functions and activities.

One of the students challenged my suggestion that our thoughts and feelings are projected to those around us and will likewise result in an increased return of good or ill. He and his companions volunteered to conduct an experiment to prove that I was mistaken about such things. I invited them to bring their results to the concluding session two weeks later.

When they returned, they sketched briefly on the blackboard a diagram of their experiment. They had taken a piece of heavy plank, and on top of it they had mounted a seismograph. Underneath they had suspended a sonar sounding device like that used on ships to detect underwater disturbances.

They placed this equipment well out in one of their man-made lakes. Then they took a large boulder and threw it so it landed in the water near this device. The seismograph registered the splash, the waves, and even the ripples as they disappeared along the shoreline.

The students continued to focus their binoculars on the seismograph. In a little while the recording needle began to move in an ever-increasing intensity. The monitoring tape showed the final register to be almost three times the intensity of the register of the splash. They concluded that the ripples to the shoreline had returned under water back to the rock, the original source of the energy. The sonar system in the water indicated that the force that returned to the rock had been multiplied approximately three times.

They concluded that since this principle applies to inanimate objects (such as the rock), it would surely apply to thoughts and feelings, which scientific instruments have recorded as producing measurable amounts of energy.

We can learn this for ourselves. All we have to do is to be in the same room with someone who is angry, to feel the energy he is radiating, which is being absorbed by our nervous systems. Thus, through negative radiation, we deplete each other and insulate ourselves from the Spirit of the Lord. The person generating such anger is greatly harmed as this negative energy multiplies and returns to be reabsorbed by his own soul.

For that which ye do send out shall return unto you again. (Alma 41:15.)

Whatever you give to life will return to you — multiplied! This applies to our daily thoughts, feelings, and actions, be they positive or negative, uplifting or depressing. Hence, we need to make wise decisions.

Because of this principle, you can make for yourself a heaven or a hell on earth. You alone must bear the responsibility for the choices you make.

Who sets the standard of what forgiveness you may expect to receive? You do. (Matthew 6:14-15.) If you wish to be forgiven, you must first forgive others.

Who sets the standard of how you will be judged? You do. (Matthew 7:1-2.) Your own judgment by your Heavenly Father will be compassionate or harsh, depending upon what standard you have set in judging others.

The things you desire from life, you must first give to life. (Matthew 7:12.) What about acquiring the things you want? Like the seed planted in the ground, life can only return to you that which you first have given — with the added promise that everything you give must ultimately return to you multiplied. Perhaps that is why a sage of bygone years said a great truth, "Give to the world the best that you have and the best will come back to you." And we might add, it will be multiplied!

If you feel that you are accident-prone, or a "worry wart," or a "Why-does-this-always-happen-to-me" sort of person, you have become a victim rather than a master of this law. Your attention is on your troubles and because of this they will continue to multiply. But this law can work for you as well as against you.

In the Bible, Job is the epitome of a just and perfect man with many problems. At the beginning of his record it appears that he did not understand the implications of the Law of the Harvest.

As a young person in Sunday School, it used to bother me a great deal when our teacher related to us the story of Job and his excruciating suffering and pain. The explanation was always that we must be patient in our afflictions and sufferings, just like Job.

The rationalization was always that the devil wanted to test Job and that God gave him the privilege of literally wrecking this poor man's life and everything he had built up. I could never accept that kind of a God, one who would compromise or "make a deal" with the devil. My experience has confirmed to me that he is a God of love, a God of kindness, a God of patience, my Father who is divine and has placed me here upon this earth so that I might have joy. I could not conceive of his deliberately permitting this type of suffering to happen to a perfect person.

After reading the biblical account many times, it finally occurred to me that Job tells the real cause of all his disasters in the third chapter, twenty-fifth verse: "For the thing which I greatly feared is come upon me, and that which I was afraid of is come unto me." (Job 3:25.)

In other words, Job acknowledged that he was afraid, that he was a worrier. What would he do if he lost his health? What would he do if he lost his possessions? What would he do if he lost his business? What would he do if he lost his house? What would happen if he lost some of his loved ones? What would happen if he lost his entire family? What would happen if his closest friends turned against him? Such thoughts, apparently, preyed on him continually.

The law is that the things which we think and the things which we harbor generate our feelings, and these feelings result in our acts which produce the harvest. For "whatsoever a man soweth, that shall he also reap." (Galatians 6:7.) "For as [a man] thinketh in his heart, so is he." (Proverbs 23:7.)

Since Job sowed seeds of worry, doubt, and fear, the devil had access to him and the harvest was calamitous. He lost everything but his faith in the Lord.

The things that Job was admittedly so much concerned about, came to pass. They became so unbearable that he wished that he had never been born, that he had been hidden under the greatest mountain chain so that not even God could find him or have any recollection of his existence.

But with all his problems and troubles, he did not deny God. Finally the Lord came to him and said, in effect, "Job, wake up and be a man. Don't you recall how happy you were in the morn of creation and how eagerly you looked forward to the wonderful opportunity of coming to this earth and partaking of the beauties here? Now stop whining and be a man. Gird up your loins and speak as if thou hast understanding."

When Job perceived the message and realized that he had sown the seeds of his own problems and undoing, he took on new courage. (Job 42.) He then departed from fear and desired the things which are of God. He was eager to follow the guidelines that the Lord had given him. Note how the Law of the Harvest began to work for his benefit when he changed his attitude.

The scriptures reveal that when Job realized the cause of his dilemma and asked the Lord's forgiveness, his blessings were multiplied abundantly; he was rewarded two-fold in family, in friends, in flocks and herds, in health, and in all that makes for an abundant life.

Since I became aware of the cause of Job's real problem, it has always been my feeling that his patience and long-suffering provide comfort and hope for those who suffer similar afflictions for the same reasons. It also teaches us to "hang in there" until we learn the means by which we can move in the other direction. However, the underlying message seems to be that we should profit from Job's experience. By recognizing and applying those laws and keys which Job, after his problems, learned to recognize and apply, spiritual calamities may be avoided and we can wake up and live.

Whatever we emanate in our thoughts, feelings, or actions will return to us multiplied manyfold!

Law of Agency and Accountability

The second principle is the Law of Agency and Accountability.

Agency is a gift from God. We can choose.

While many people throughout the world recognize that man is a creation who has the right of choice, the Holy Bible does not mention it clearly as a right given us by God. It appears to be one of those "plain and precious things" (1 Nephi 13:28.) that was removed from the Bible. Without the aid of latter-day revelation, the world as a whole would have little awareness of the crucial ramifications of this principle of agency and its attendant responsibility.

We know that Moses understood that people could choose. (Deuteronomy 30:19.)

No mention, however, is made in Genesis of Adam's receiving the freedom to choose from God. And modern revelation clarifies this matter. (Moses 3:17.)

The book of Moses establishes the fact that the agency of man is a gift from God. We need this recognition as a base.

> . . . Satan rebelled against me, and sought to destroy the agency of man, which I, the Lord God, had given him. . . . (Moses 4:3.)

God will not and the devil cannot violate our agency.

The Prophet Joseph Smith clarified this matter:

> He then observed that Satan was generally blamed for the evils which we did, but if he was the cause of all our wickedness, men could not be condemned. The devil could not compel mankind to do evil; all was voluntary. Those who resisted the Spirit of God, would be liable to be led into temptation, and then the association of heaven would be withdrawn from those who refused to be made partakers of such great glory. God would not exert any compulsory means, and the devil could not. (*Journal of Discourses* 2:272. Hereinafter referred to as *JD*.)

Brigham Young also taught this principle: "The volition of the creature is free; this is a law of their existence, and the Lord cannot violate his own law; were He to do that, He would cease to be God." (*JD* 2:272.)

If God will not and the devil cannot violate our agency, why should we allow others to dictate our thoughts, feelings, or actions?

We are accountable for our own choices.

The inherent accountability that attends this gift of agency is plainly set forth in the Doctrine and Covenants: "That every man may act in doctrine and principle pertaining to futurity, according to the moral agency which I have given unto him, that every man may be accountable for his own sins in the day of judgment." (D&C 101:78.)

Some people may feel that the atonement of Jesus Christ absolves us from responsibility for our sins. Not so! Jesus Christ declared, "For behold, I, God, have suffered these things for all, that they might not suffer if they would repent; But if they would not repent, They must suffer even as I." (D&C 19:16-17.)

This implies that so far as our sins are concerned, the Atonement is not unconditional. It is true that Jesus died for our sins, but only upon one condition: if we repent.

If we do not repent, the Law of the Harvest will work against us. What we sow that is contrary to God's laws, we will reap in suffering, bitterness, and sorrow. In this manner we literally become the maker of our own destiny.

But you may say, "What about the devil's great power?"

If you read the small print in the scriptures — the part that is rarely emphasized — you will often find an "if," "when," "because," or "as you permit it" clause. (Alma 5:20; Mosiah 16:3; D&C 19:16-17; Alma 39:11; 3 Nephi 7:5; D&C 76:31; 2 Nephi 26:10.)

Brigham Young's counselor, Heber C. Kimball, issued this challenge:

> I do not fear any thing. I fear nothing that is in heaven, or that is upon the earth. I do not fear hell nor its combinations; neither hell, nor the devil, nor any of his angels has power over me, or over you only as we permit them to have.
>
> If we permit the devil to have power over us . . . then will he have dominion over us. Upon the same principle, we let sin have power over us, but it has no power over us unless we subject ourselves to it. (*JD* 1:204.)

You cannot be justified by saying, "The devil made me do it." What you must really mean is "I permitted the devil to influence me and I fell for it."

Since we are free to choose and are accountable for our choices, it is obvious that in our own best self-interest we should always choose the right.

Two Keys to Self-Mastery

In addition to these two important principles — the Law of

the Harvest and the Law of Agency and Accountability — there are two keys which can change your life and contribute greatly toward your reaching your goal of self-mastery.

Key Number One: We Must Be Positive

The first key to remember is that God works through positive thoughts, feelings, and acts. The adversary enters our lives through negative thoughts, feelings, and acts.

President George Albert Smith was taught this principle as a young child.

> There are two influences in the world today, and have been from the beginning. One is an influence that is constructive, that radiates happiness, and builds character. The other influence is one that destroys, turns men into demons, tears down and discourages. We are all susceptible to both. The one comes from our Heavenly Father, and the other comes from the source of evil that has been in the world from the beginning, seeking to bring about the destruction of the human family.
>
> My grandfather used to say to his family, "There is a line of demarcation, well defined, between the Lord's territory and the devil's. If you will stay on the Lord's side of the line you will be under his influence and will have no desire to do wrong; but if you cross to the devil's side of the line one inch, you are in the tempter's power, and if he is successful, you will not be able to think or even reason properly, because you will have lost the spirit of the Lord. . . .
>
> If you want to be happy, remember that all happiness worthy of the name is on the Lord's side of the line and all sorrow and disappointment is on the devil's side of the line. (*Sharing the Gospel With Others* [Salt Lake City: Deseret News Press, 1948], pp. 42-43.)

The Apostle Paul discusses the same principle in Galatians. He identifies positive feelings as "fruits of the Spirit" and negative feelings and works as "works of the flesh." (Galatians 5:19.)

Dr. John A. Widtsoe explained: "The devil is subject to God, and is allowed to operate only if he keeps within well-defined limits. . . ." (*A Rational Theology* [Salt Lake City: General Priesthood Committee, 1915], p. 81.)

God works through positive thoughts, feelings, and acts. The devil works through negative thoughts, feelings, and acts.

The scriptures affirm this fact. Notice what they say.

Examples of feelings that come from God are found in the following scriptures: love—1 Thessalonians 4:9; 1 John 2:10; D&C 76:116; D&C 121:41; humility—Matthew 18:4; James 4:10; 1 Peter 5:6; D&C 112:10; thankfulness—Psalm 100:4; Ephesians 5:17, 20; D&C 46:7; 78:19; forgiveness—Matthew 6:14-15; Mark 11:25; Mosiah 26:30; D&C 64:7-11.

Conversely, the following are examples of scriptures that describe the negative feelings of Satan: fear—2 Timothy 1:7; Joshua 1:9; Revelation 21:8; D&C 6:36; anger—Psalm 37:8; Matthew 5:22; Moroni 9:3; 2 Nephi 33:5; D&C 10:24; unbelief— Revelation 21:8; Hebrews 3:12; Matthew 13:58; D&C 58:15; contention—3 Nephi 11:29; D&C 10:63; Luke 6:30 (JST).

God's Side	Love
	Rejoicing (praise)
	Thankfulness (gratitude)
	Joy
	Faith
	Forgiveness
	Patience (longsuffering)
	Humility (meekness)
	Harmony
	Peace
	Temperance
	Goodness
	Gentleness

————————————————THE LINE————————————————

Adversary's Side	Faultfinding (criticism)
	Discord (quarrel)
	Contention (argument)
	Pride (dispute)
	Envy
	Discouragement
	Disbelief (doubt)
	Fear (worry, anxiety)
	Anger
	Hate

Ask yourself, "Am I on the Lord's side of the line?" You will probably find that your answer will change as conditions change.

Do not be discouraged, because you can control the situation. The above chart is only a beginning.

Many scriptures confirm this principle. The following is a partial list:

Virtues (positive side of the line): 2 Peter 1:5-8; Article of Faith 13; Deuteronomy 6:5-7; Joshua 1:9; 2 Nephi 31:20; Psalm 24:3-5; 1 Thessalonians 5:14-22; Mosiah 26:39; Matthew 5:44, 6:33, 7:7; D&C 112:10; 78:19; 121:41-45.

Sins (negative side of the line): Romans 1:24-32; 1 Corinthians 3:16-17; 6:1-10; 10:8; Ephesians 5:3-7; Galatians 5:19-21; Colossians 3:5, 7-8; 1 Thessalonians 4:3-5; Revelation 21:8.

Everyone knows that he or she should not be filled with anger, hate, jealousy, or similar feelings. But do we also recognize that we should not be worried, or afraid, or feel sorry for or be critical of ourselves? Do we realize that doubting is the principal cause of many of our troubles?

In Revelation 21:8 special emphasis is given to unbelief. In Mormon 9:23-29 a special discourse by Moroni contrasts belief and doubting.

A fascinating discourse I have discovered on this subject discusses the virtue of faith versus the sin of doubt. I am including it herewith because it is not generally available to many people.

> Remove from thee all doubting;
> And question nothing at all,
>   when thou asketh anything of the Lord;
> Saying within thyself: how shall I be able
>   to ask anything of the Lord and receive it,
> Seeing I have so greatly sinned against him?
>
> Do not think thus, but turn unto the Lord
>   with all thy heart,
> And ask of him without doubting . . .
>
> Wherefore purify thy heart from all the vices
>   of this present world;
> And thou shalt receive whatsoever good things
>   thou shalt ask,
> And nothing shall be wanting unto thee
>   of all thy petitions;
> If thou shalt ask of the Lord without doubting . . .

But they that are not such, shall obtain
    none of those things which they ask,
For they that are full of faith ask all things
    with confidence and receive from the Lord
Because they ask without doubting . . .

Wherefore, purify thy heart from doubting,
And put on faith, and trust in God,
and thou shalt receive all that thou shalt ask.

But if thou shouldest chance to ask somewhat
    and not (immediately) receive it,
Yet do not therefore doubt, because thou hast not
    presently received the petition of thy soul . . .

But do not leave off to ask, and then thou shalt receive.
Else if thou shalt cease to ask, thou must complain
    of thyself, and not of God,
That he has not given unto thee what thou didst desire.

Consider therefore this doubting,
    how cruel and pernicious it is;
And how it utterly roots out many from the faith,
    who were very faithful and firm.
For this doubting is the daughter of the devil,
    and deals very wickedly with the servants of God.

Despise it, therefore, and thou shalt rule over it
    on every occasion.
Put on a firm and powerful faith;
For faith promises all things and perfects all things,
But doubting will not believe that it shall
    obtain anything, by all that it can do.

Faith cometh from above, from God;
    and hath great power.
But doubting is an earthly spirit,
    and proceedeth from the devil,
And has no strength.

Do thou therefore keep the virtue of faith,
And depart from doubting, in which is no virtue,
And thou shalt live unto God.
(2 Hermas 9:1-11, *The Lost Books of the Bible* [Cleveland: World
Publishing Company, 1926], pp. 221-22. Taken from the *Pseudepi-
grapha*, published in 1911.)

Negative feelings and attitudes can effectively stop the Spirit of the Lord and the influence of the Holy Ghost from flowing through us with their healing power, sanctifying influence, inspiration, and blessing.

The Holy Ghost cannot dwell where there is discord. He works on God's side of the line. He cannot dwell in an unclean body, and he will not abide in a mind or heart that harbors negative influences of any kind.

Love, as Jesus outlined it, fulfills all the law and the prophets.

> Thou shalt love the Lord thy God with all thy heart, and with all thy soul, and with all thy mind.
> This is the first and great commandment.
> And the second is like unto it, thou shalt love thy neighbor as thyself.
> On these two commandments hang all the law and the prophets. (Matthew 22:37-40.)

Of course it does. Love keeps you on God's side of the line where all the blessings are. Obviously, love is the most important single quality of character that we are to develop and practice in our lives.

To the extent that you genuinely love God, you cannot help but become more like him. (Nathaniel Hawthorne's story of *The Great Stone Face* is an excellent example of what happens when a person keeps his mind on an ideal.) As you develop this love, you are then able to share it with others. You cannot share something with others that you yourself do not possess. By sharing this love through serving your fellowmen, it will multiply and return to increase your own love until it reaches divine proportions, exemplifying the principle of the Law of the Harvest. With the foundation of such divine love, it will be a joy to love your neighbor as yourself!

Faith, inspiration, healing, personal revelation, and priesthood power, as well as patience, forgiveness, and other Godlike virtues, are all from the same source as love. This is the way to perfection.

The same base of spiritual receptiveness applies to all of the gifts of the Spirit. No matter what gifts of the Spirit we may have been promised or may have received, the fruits of these gifts will not be made manifest unless we are on the Lord's side of the line.

When we are on the negative side — the devil's side — we will not be receptive to positive inspiration any more than we could hear an FM radio program while tuned in on the AM band.

The Spirit of the Lord is not imposed upon us. We have to be receptive first before receiving its indwelling power.

Key Number Two: We Can Change

The second key to remember is that we can choose to change. Most of us realize that we can choose our actions and our words. But do we also realize that we can choose our thoughts and our feelings as well? We do not have to be "driven with the wind and tossed" if we do not want to be.

Thoughts are powerful things. Our thoughts generate our feelings. Our feelings motivate our actions. Our actions lead to our accomplishments or failures. The following scripture verifies this fact: ". . . whosoever looketh on a woman to lust after her hath committed adultery with her already in his heart." (Matthew 5:28.)

It follows, then, that we can control our feelings by controlling our thoughts. And we can usually control our thoughts by controlling the focus of our attention. And unless we do so, we become the victims rather than the masters of these laws.

The problem arises when we do not realize that the ability to choose to change ourselves is part of the divine endowment of our agency. We do not have to worry or be afraid. Yet we spend much of our lives suffering, being fearful and discouraged, and nursing hurt feelings.

Why do we do this? We are living in an environment that is saturated with negative thoughts and feelings, and they are contagious! Consider for a moment our newspapers, magazines, television programs, and conversations. Do most of them lift our hearts and our spirits?

A random sampling of your daily newspaper will give you a clue. We examined the first section of our daily paper to see what we would find. Out of 44 columns of print that were analyzed, 41.8 were negative and only 2.2 were positive. That is approximately 5 percent positive.

If you spend sixty minutes a day on such material, it means that fifty-seven minutes are spent in a negative environment and only three minutes in a positive environment. Considering our newspaper's 786,762 advertised subscribers, approximately 39,000 hours were spent in positive reading and 748,000 hours in negative exposure. That makes a ratio of 19 to 1 in favor of negativity.

What a way to start each new day! And remember that all these people will be sharing their negatively-influenced thoughts and feelings with others for the rest of the day.

Examining some other media will yield similar results. Small wonder that this poses a real challenge for all of us who want to stay on the Lord's side — the positive side — of the line.

We can stay on the Lord's side of the line! But we must choose to do so. We must learn how to do it. We must practice doing it.

This is where attunement with the Spirit is possible. This is where faith is exercised. This is where healing occurs. This is where divine revelation can come to us. This is where the power of God can be manifest in our lives. This is where we can receive inspiration to solve our problems.

We need positive thoughts and feelings to have the help of the Lord.

Once we learn this principle and practice it, we realize that we can control our feelings; we are then on the road to over- coming negativity.

One of the highlights of your life will be the day that you, being discouraged, lonely, depressed, and worried, succeed in turning yourself around so the Spirit of the Lord can flood your soul.

When we are living on the negative side of the line — in the devil's territory — problems will multiply. Whether they be health problems, financial problems, or relationship problems, they all result from the fact that we are wallowing in negation, and we do not realize that we do not have to feel that way. We can change our feelings.

If you find yourself to be fearful, at least you are in good company. How did Moses handle it? Joseph Smith? Job? Nephi?

Moses continued calling upon the Lord for strength until he had sufficient for his need. (Moses 1:12-22.)

Joseph Smith was a boy. He exerted all his powers in calling upon God to deliver him from the enemy, and he was rescued. (Joseph Smith—History 1:15-17.)

Job repented. (Job 42:3-6.)

Nephi talked aloud about his fears and his love and trust in God. (2 Nephi 4:16-35.)

You can do all of this, too. I know of a sister who was having serious trouble with a teenage son. One day she had a call to come to school about more problems. On the way home she was so preoccupied with her worries that she had a minor car accident. Now she was really depressed!

Then she remembered how Nephi had handled similar depression. *Why am I feeling this way?* she asked herself. *I don't have to feel this way.* She prayed that these feelings would be taken from her and that she would be filled with the Spirit of the Lord. Within a few minutes she was happy, filled with peace in her heart, and was in a position to receive inspiration regarding her problems. She said it was a thrilling experience to see how her feelings had changed so quickly and to realize that she was able to do something about them.

We Can Change Our Feelings By Changing Our Thoughts

When you find yourself feeling depressed, worried, or fearful, realize that you are "below the line" and that if you stay there things will become worse. But you can pull yourself above the line. Nephi did it. And so can you!

The minute you change your attention from your troubles, such as praying for help, counting your blessings, or rebuking your negative feelings, you have opened the door for the Spirit of the Lord to help you.

With all the negative influences around us, we need to do something to counteract them. The scriptures are filled with timely counsel to help us maintain a positive attitude. This counsel isn't preaching. Its message is vital to our eternal welfare —how to keep our feelings on the positive side of the line. For example, here are four different ways:

Pray: pray unto him continually. (2 Nephi 9:52.)
Search: search the scriptures. (John 5:39.)

Feast: feast upon the words of Christ. (2 Nephi 32:3.)
Thank: he who receiveth all things with thankfulness.
           (D&C 78:19.)

If we would just do these things consistently, we would be protected automatically. Our hearts and minds would be open to the Spirit of the Lord.

I Am! I Can! I Will!

My wife and I used to prepare periodic family bulletins. These were a means of "acceptable preaching" for our children as they became young adults and lived in various parts of the nation. On the right side of the heading was a sign: I am! I can! I will! And below was the inscription: ". . . as for me and my house, we will serve the Lord." (Joshua 24:15.)

An important factor was the realization that until we eagerly say "I will" to ourselves and others, we do not make a commitment for success. Such statements as "I'll consider it" or "I'll try" are usually nothing more than excuses for failure.

We feel that this is one reason why the Savior offered us such noble challenges as "be ye perfect," "be ye holy," "be ye even as I am," and "come, follow me."

If we commit ourselves to reach a higher plane, we can do it by applying all these principles and keys wisely, and with God's help. As our beloved prophet, Spencer W. Kimball, has advised, "Do it!" Repeat the following to yourself:

> I am a son or daughter of God.
> I am of divine parentage.
> Because I am, there are certain things expected of me.
> Because I am, I can do them!
> And because I am and I can do them,
> I will!

Never again, as long as you exist, should you knowingly use your power of creation to plant seeds that will warp or destroy your life, your happiness and joy, and the lives of others. Your challenge is to build. In the Savior's words,

Ye are the salt of the earth. Ye are the light of the world. (Matthew 5:13-14.)

3

Ever keep in exercise the principle
of mercy, and be ready to forgive
our brother on the first intimations
of repentance, and asking forgiveness;
and should we even forgive our brother,
or even our enemy, before he repents
or asks forgiveness, our Heavenly
Father would be equally as merciful
unto us.
(DHC 5:41)

Dissolving Resentments and Achieving Forgiveness

Accumulated resentments are warping or destroying the lives of millions of people in this land and in other countries around the world. Resentments are insidious by nature. They generally create greater havoc with the one who harbors them than with the person or persons against whom such resentment is focused.

As long as we cling to resentments, we short-circuit the glorious regenerating power of forgiveness in our own lives and delay its benign influence in the lives of those against whom resentment is focused.

The Key to Well-Being

In considering this vital subject, let us remember that love is the fulfilling of all the law and the prophets. (Matthew 22:40.) To overcome resentments requires Christlike love. Out of love grow gratitude, thanksgiving, kindness, tenderness, humility, meekness, joy, and, above all else, forgiveness. These are all godly virtues through which we can be lifted up. We can have increased light until there is no darkness in us. ". . . and that body which is filled with light comprehendeth all things." (D&C 88:67.) What a glorious promise!

On the other hand, doubt, worry, anxiety, fear, hate, bickering, strife, disputation, contention, fault-finding, and resentments come from the evil one. They are on his side of the line! They have no association with faith. They have no relevance with trust. They are the antithesis of love. Recall how the Apostle Paul emphasized this fact to Timothy: "For God hath not given us the spirit of fear; but of power, and of love, and of a sound mind." (2 Timothy 1:7.)

We cannot serve God and mammon! We cannot nurture seeds of distrust, seeds of suspicion, seeds of jealousy, and others, all of which stem from doubt. If we do, we deny ourselves the power of God that can operate in and through us. We cannot serve two masters.

Have you ever wondered why you did not receive a blessing you desired?

> Ye endeavored to believe that ye should receive the blessing which was offered unto you; but behold . . . there were fears in your hearts, and . . . this is the reason that ye did not receive. (D&C 67:3.)

We must rid our minds, our thoughts, our feelings, and our actions of all negative qualities. By entertaining or cultivating such negativity in our lives, we are opening the door to the adversary and relinquishing our divine strength and power to be used by him for his avowed purpose—our misery and ultimate destruction. (2 Nephi 2:27.)

The Power of Forgiveness

One day at the Church offices, I was walking down the hall when President Levi Edgar Young motioned for me to come into his office. As I entered he invited me to be seated and said, "Brother Babbel, if you have a few minutes I would like to share with you a lovely experience I have just had."

As I sat down he said, "Did you happen to notice that elderly gentleman whom I just helped into the elevator?" I replied affirmatively.

Then President Young related to me the following experience. That man, who appeared to be in his eighties, had approached him earlier that afternoon, and President Young had detected from the man's broken English that he was of Germanic origin.

"Are you President Young?" he queried. "Levi Edgar Young?" came his next question. President Young responded affirmatively to both inquiries.

"Were you ever a missionary for your Church?" President Young informed him that he had been engaged in several missions.

"Were you ever a missionary in Germany?"

"Yes, I served a mission in Germany," came the reply. "In fact, that was my first mission. I was about nineteen years old."

"Did you ever labor in the city of Leipzig?"

"Yes, that was my first field of labor."

Then this elderly man continued: "Do you remember a time when you were tracting on the third floor of an apartment building? As you attempted to give a man one of your tracts and a brief message, he became very angry. He struck you, threw you down the stairs, and continued to maul you until you reached the street, where he left you lying in the gutter bruised and bleeding. Do you remember that?"

President Young said that he had to ponder this question for some time before he could remember it.

With tears coursing down his aged cheeks, this man dropped to his knees and pleaded: "President Young. I am that man. I have waited for over fifty years for this day that I might come here and ask your forgiveness for what I did to you at that time. I did accept your message later and became a member of the Church. Since then I have tried to do what is right. I have come here now to ask your forgiveness."

After gaining control of his own feelings, President Young responded, "Of course, dear Brother. I forgive you. Don't you remember that I turned and forgave you while I was lying in the gutter?"

Then President Young continued: "Brother Babbel, because I honestly forgave that man as sincerely as Jesus forgave those who maligned him while he hung on the cross, the memory of that event had been taken from me completely. Until this good Brother brought it to my attention, it had never crossed my mind."

Then he shared with me this sterling counsel: "This is one of the great lessons we have to learn in life. The Lord has said, 'I, the Lord, will forgive whom I will forgive, but of you it is required to forgive all men.' (D&C 64:10.) It is pleasing to him if we forgive the moment that such an incident occurs.

"When this is done," he concluded, "the load is lifted from you and the healing influence can go from you to make the matter right. On the other hand, if that person who was guilty of the offense does not seek forgiveness, he will carry a burden that will weigh him down and become more distressing with each passing year. What compassion I feel for this elderly brother who has lived with his tormented conscience for over fifty years!"

The Curse of Resentments

Later when I was living in the Portland, Oregon, area, an urgent call came from a valued friend who had been bedfast for nearly a year. Now his condition was critical.

When I reached his home, I found him resting on his front room couch. His wife was in the adjoining dining room, ironing his burial clothes.

He told me that his family doctor had informed him earlier that afternoon that his life was nearing its end and that it was now only a matter of a day or two, or perhaps a week at the most, until he would expire. Then he remarked: "The strange thing about this whole matter is that the doctors still do not know what is wrong with me. They just know that I am dying. Tonight I just felt that I wanted to visit with you before I prepare to meet my Maker."

While continuing our conversation, I received a divine insight as to what his real problem was. "Brother," I responded, "I believe I know what is wrong."

He seemed startled, but genuinely interested, as he urged, "Please tell me."

"You've had a number of very serious hurts and disappointments in your life," I said, "that have filled you with bitter resentment. Many of these have never been resolved."

He seemed incredulous and somewhat apprehensive as he inquired, "What do you know about them?"

"Not a thing," I replied, "unless you tell me about them. I only perceive that you have been deeply hurt many times. Yet you have never forgiven those who were responsible for these offenses."

"Well, I must admit," he countered, "that I have had some pretty bitter experiences. But since I accepted the gospel, I believe that I could forgive those who were responsible if they asked for my forgiveness."

"But that is not how the principle of forgiveness works," I said. "When any serious grievance takes place, the Lord requires us to forgive the guilty party the moment the infraction occurs, if possible."

I related to my friend the experience that President Levi Edgar Young had shared with me earlier. I could tell that he was beginning to get the message. I inquired whether or not he had ever visited the rattlesnake farm near Salem, Oregon, where they extract venom and process small cans of rattlesnake meat for venturesome gourmets. He said he had heard of the farm but had not been there.

"Recently I heard of an experiment that was conducted there," I said. "One of the caretakers took one of his large rattlesnakes and put a forked stick behind its head so it could not coil to strike. Then he began to tantalize it with small chicks and other food. The snake kept trying to coil unsuccessfully, and venom dripped quite freely from its fangs. Within minutes the snake stiffened and died.

"The caretaker then commented that a rattlesnake can stand just about anything except its own venom. When it cannot discharge the venom as fast as it is produced, it dies of its own accumulated poison."

Then I suggested to my friend that his own condition somewhat paralleled that of the snake: "When you have any resentment, hurt, bitterness, or hatred in your heart, regardless of the cause, if you do not get rid of it at once through the spirit of forgiveness, the hatred will continue to fester and grow and increase, since that is the basic Law of the Harvest. Unless contained, these negative feelings will finally consume and destroy the person who harbors them. This is what has been troubling you and what, even now, has brought you to the point of death."

My friend began to sob unashamedly. In the process he removed his nightshirt and showed me his bare back. I had never seen a back like this, not even in the concentration camps of Europe. Across his back were large criss-crossed scars that were scabbed over with ugly flesh. Some of them were so deep a person could almost lay his arm in them.

Then he related to me how his father used to come home occasionally in a mean, drunken stupor. His temper would flare up and he would take a heavy whip from the wall and flog whoever was within reach. This whip, a "cat o' nine tails," was leather with several strands. At the end of each strand was fastened a large brass ball with metal spikes that could tear the hide off an animal.

On one occasion my friend was the victim. Just fourteen years old at the time, he was whipped into unconsciousness. How long he lay on the floor he did not know, but as he regained consciousness, he found himself lying in a pool of his own blood, with his back fairly torn to shreds. He managed somehow to crawl from his house, and he vowed he would never return.

At this point I interrupted, "You've kept that promise, haven't you?"

"Yes," he replied.

"You've never forgiven your father for that flogging, have you?" I next inquired.

"No, I guess not," was his reply. "But if dad were to ask for my forgiveness, I think I could forgive him now."

"I'm concerned," I said, "that you still don't understand the underlying principle. You have had the divine responsibility of forgiving your father from the moment that you regained consciousness, so that the healing power of forgiveness could come into your own life and relieve you of this terrible burden. In doing so, you might also have started the process of healing for your father as well. But because you have continued to nurture this resentment, it has festered and grown until it is literally consuming you. In addition, I feel you still have a number of other resentments against others that likewise have never been resolved. These are adding to your burden and hastening your untimely death."

My friend then recalled numerous other cases throughout Canada, Montana, and the Pacific Northwest, none of which had been resolved.

"Where does your father live?" I asked next.

"The last I knew, he was living in North Dakota," my friend responded. "I haven't seen him or been in touch with him for over forty years."

When we finished talking, I invited him to sit upon a chair so I could give him a special blessing and outline for him what must be done. In the blessing he was instructed to get out of bed the following morning, take his wife, and drive to his father's home in North Dakota, with the assurance that his father was still alive. He was also to drive to the homes of all the other people against whom he had resentments, no matter where they lived.

In each case he was to ask for their forgiveness for having harbored resentments against them. "Don't go there and try to persuade them to beg for your forgiveness," I admonished. "Rather, your assignment is to ask their forgiveness for your having failed to make a reconciliation these many years." The blessing outlined how he was to ask for such forgiveness. In addition, I blessed him with the necessary strength to accomplish this task successfully.

About four or five weeks later my friend stopped his car in our driveway. As he stepped out of his car, I greeted him with, "Brother, you're a well man now, aren't you?"

"Yes," he responded, "I haven't felt this good in many years."

He then began to relate to me his experiences. He told me about meeting his aged father, who was now in his eighties and nearly blind. When his father came to the door, he inquired in his usual gruff manner, "Who are you?"

My friend informed him that he was his son. Still rather brusquely, his father responded, "Well, what do you want now?"

My friend answered: "Dad, I have come home to ask for your forgiveness. For years I have held a bitter resentment against you for what you did to me when I was a young man. I had no right to feel resentment toward you. Can you forgive me for holding a grudge all these years?"

He said that his father looked stunned for a moment. Then he broke down and cried, threw his arms around his son, and sobbed, "Son, I'm the one who should have asked for your forgiveness, but I didn't have the courage. Can you forgive me?"

Then my friend added: "You know, we made a complete reconciliation. The spirit of peace and forgiveness flooded both of our lives. I had a similar experience in every home I visited, as you directed me to do in my blessing. Today I am a happy, healthy man. I'm at peace with myself and with my Lord."

Within six months my friend was the third-highest sales producer for the large life insurance company he represented. Just before Christmas he and his wife were called to go on a special mission to New Zealand. More than thirty years later, as far as I am aware, he is still very much alive, enjoying life and serving his fellowmen — this man who was doomed to die in 1951!

Challenges and Benefits

These events have had a profound influence in my own life and in the lives of many others. This principle of forgiveness is so vital that we should be overjoyed to put it into daily use.

When we really understand and practice the principle of forgiveness as the Lord outlined it, we will be doubly blessed. First, we will be freed from the burden of accumulated resentments that continually multiply and fester when harbored in our hearts. Second, we will activate the principle of forgiveness in our own lives. Unless and until we forgive others, the divine law specifies that there is no forgiveness for us, for we must be measured by the precedent we have established in our forgiveness of others or in our own lack of forgiveness. Third, we will hasten the principle's purifying influence in the lives of those against whom our resentment is focused.

This, then, is the standard by which we shall be measured:

> . . . ye ought to forgive one another; for he that forgiveth not his brother his trespasses standeth condemned before the Lord; for there remaineth in him the greater sin.
>
> I, the Lord, will forgive whom I will forgive, but of you it is required to forgive all men. (D&C 64:9-10.)

As in most matters in life, we set the standard for our own forgiveness. Since we all need forgiveness in abundance, we should welcome the opportunity to lavish it upon every living soul with whom we come in contact, including our bitterest enemies!

No one can have a happier life unless this principle is practiced daily to open the doors for our own forgiveness and to bring about the healing needed in those who have been guilty of the offense in the first place. Unless and until we do, the greater sin remains with us since we are deliberately shortchanging both parties involved.

In a very real sense, harboring resentments can contribute to our own untimely death as well as the misery of those against whom such resentments are focused.

The true spirit of forgiveness is beautifully portrayed in the following poem by Carol Lynn Pearson:

The Forgiving

Forgive?
Will I forgive,
You cry.
But
What is the gift,
The favor?

You would lift
Me from
My poor place
To stand beside
The Savior.

You would have
Me see with
His eyes,
Smile,
And with Him
Reach out to
Salve
A sorrowing heart—
For one small
Moment
To share in
Christ's great art.

Will I forgive,
You cry.
Oh,
May I—
May I?

The time will come when no man or woman will be able to endure on borrowed light.
(Orson F. Whitney, *Life of Heber C. Kimball* [Salt Lake City: Steven and Wallis, Inc., 1945], p. 461.)

4

Establishing Personal Revelation

Shortly before his passing, President Harold B. Lee declared that the above prophetic statement by Heber C. Kimball is now being fulfilled.

> The time is here when every one of you must stand on your own feet. The time is here when no man and woman will endure on borrowed light. Each will have to be guided by the light within himself. If you do not have it, you will not stand. (Harold B. Lee, *Decisions for Successful Living* [Salt Lake City: Deseret Book Co., 1973], p. 234.)

We never know when we may have urgent need for the direction of the Lord. President Brigham Young gave William Hayward a blessing in the St. George Temple, promising him the gift of healing and the answers to his prayers. Many times his prayers were answered.

At one time the Haywards were traveling from Moroni to Nephi [Utah] and were obliged to make camp in Salt Creek Canyon. Another family had camped at the same place and after they had all retired and everything seemed peaceful, William awoke. He immediately awakened the rest of the camp and told them he had had a warning of danger. They must move on. The other campers decided not to go, but William took his family and left.

During the night the rest of the camp were murdered by prowling Indians. A monument was erected to their memory and still stands in Salt Creek Canyon. The lives of the William Hayward family were spared. (*Life History of William Hayward*, comp. ReVon Hayward Porter [Unpublished manuscript].)

It is vital that each person should understand the principle of individual divine revelation and how to obtain it. The Prophet Joseph Smith's counsel is especially pertinent:

The best way to obtain truth and wisdom is not to ask it from books, but to go to God in prayer, and obtain divine teaching . . . There is never a time when the spirit is too old to approach God. (Joseph Smith, *Teachings of the Prophet Joseph Smith*, 3rd ed., sel. Joseph Fielding Smith [Salt Lake City: Deseret News Press, 1942], p. 191. Hereinafter referred to as *TPJS*.)

The power of the Holy Ghost, which includes the spirit of revelation, can expand in our lives and open the door to such divine teaching.

Why Should We Desire Personal Revelation?

We have a right to receive it. President Wilford Woodruff explained:

Every man or woman that has ever entered into the Church of God and been baptized for the remission of sins, has a right to revelation, a right to the Spirit of God, to assist them in their labors, in their administrations to their children, in counseling their children and those over whom they are called upon to preside. The Holy Ghost is not restricted to men, nor to apostles, or prophets: it belongs to every faithful man and woman and to every child who is old enough to receive the gospel of Christ. (*Millennial Star*, 51:548.)

We need personal revelation daily. President John Taylor commented:

There is not a position that we can occupy in life, either as fathers, mothers, children, masters, servants, or as elders of Israel holding the holy priesthood in all its ramifications, but what we need continually is wisdom flowing from the Lord and intelligence communicated by him, that we may know how to perform correctly the various duties and avocations of life, and to fulfill the various responsibilities that rest upon us. And hence the necessity all the day long, and every day and every week, month, and year, and under all circumstances, of men leaning upon the Lord and being guided by that Spirit that flows from him, that we may not fall into error - that we may neither do anything wrong, nor think anything wrong, and all the time retain virtue, and living continually in obedience to the laws and commandments of God.

There is not a man upon the earth that has put his trust in God, I do not care what part of the world he has been in, but what can say that he delivered him. (John Taylor, *The Gospel Kingdom,* comp. G. Homer Durham [Salt Lake City: Deseret Book Co., 2nd ed., 1944], pp. 44-45.)

Fundamental Considerations

We must learn to recognize how divine direction feels! We must be able to identify it.

When we are confirmed after baptism, we are told to receive the Holy Ghost. This is the first commandment given us as members of the Church of Jesus Christ. Many people assume, because they have been told to receive the Holy Ghost, that this gift automatically vitalizes their lives. Others also presume that they always retain this gift. But the Doctrine and Covenants declares:

A man may receive the Holy Ghost, and it may descend upon him and not tarry with him. (D&C 130:23.)

President Joseph F. Smith clarifies why this is so.

. . . it will depend upon the worthiness of him unto whom the gift [of the Holy Ghost] is bestowed whether he receive the Holy Ghost or not. (*Improvement Era,* 12:390.)

The Prophet Joseph Smith gave us an important key:

No man can receive the Holy Ghost without receiving revelation. The Holy Ghost is a revelator. (*DHC* 6:58.)

Do you realize what this implies? If you have not had divine revelation in your life, you may not have received the Holy Ghost.

We cannot know the things of God except through the Spirit of God. (1 Corinthians 2:11, Joseph Smith translation.) That Spirit is the Holy Ghost.

We cannot enter into the kingdom of God without the purifying help of the Holy Ghost. (John 3:5.)

We cannot have a remission of our sins without "fire and . . . the Holy Ghost." (2 Nephi 31:17.) Obviously we not only want a remission of our sins, but also we need such a blessing urgently in our lives so we may be purified, for no unclean thing can enter the kingdom of God. (3 Nephi 27:19; 1 Nephi 10:21; 15:34; Alma 11:37; 40:26.)

We cannot know the Father or Jesus Christ without the Holy Ghost. (1 Corinthians 12:3.)

We cannot have eternal life without knowing the Father and the Son. (John 17:3.) It isn't critical how much we know *about* Jesus Christ and the Father. But it is a matter of utmost importance that we know the Father and Jesus Christ. To do so is life eternal. And the Holy Ghost is responsible for leading us to this realization.

Personal revelation needs to be activated. Reflect for a moment on these precious endowments which presently abide in you and which need the enlivening Spirit of God to bring them forth for your blessing:

> Therefore it is given to abide in you, the record of heaven, the Comforter, the peaceable things of immortal glory; the truth of all things; that which quickeneth all things; that which maketh alive all things; that which knoweth all things, and hath all power according to wisdom, mercy, truth, justice, and judgment. (Moses 6:61.)

This suggests that there is a veritable gold mine abiding within us, just awaiting the Spirit to unlock it for our benefit and spiritual growth. Evidently these qualities were gained during our premortal preparation for this mortal existence and are part of our spiritual "memory bank" held in reserve for our blessing and benefit. Unless we establish a burning desire and are in harmony with the Spirit, these most desirable endowments cannot be forthcoming.

Scope and Limitations

Let us not confuse personal revelation with seeking after signs. In our day the Lord is very specific regarding the latter.

> And he that seeketh signs shall see signs, but not unto salvation.
>
> . . . there are those among you who seek signs, and there have been such even from the beginning;
>
> But, behold, faith cometh not by signs, but signs follow those that believe.
>
> Yea, signs come by faith, unto mighty works, for without faith no man pleaseth god. . . . (D&C 63:7-9, 11.)

Does the Church have a monopoly on truth? Elder John A. Widtsoe answers this question:

> Nothing could be further from the teachings of the Church. It has been taught from the days of the Prophet Joseph Smith that the light of truth enlightens every man born into the earth. All who seek truth may find it, whether in or out of the church . . .
>
> Certainly in every church professing God there is some of this higher truth. That is the doctrine of the Latter-day Saints. ("Does Mormonism Have a Monopoly of Truth?" *Improvement Era*, Nov. 1970, p. 50.)

Presidents Brigham Young and John Taylor give additional perspective:

> I do not believe for one moment that there has been a man or woman upon the face of the earth, from the days of Adam to this day, who has not been enlightened, instructed, and taught by the revelations of Jesus Christ. "What! the ignorant heathen?" Yes, every human being who has possessed a sane mind . . .
>
> . . . Those who were honest before the Lord, and acted uprightly, according to the best knowledge they had, will have an opportunity to go into the kingdom of God. I believe this privilege belonged to the sons and daughters of Adam, and descended from him, and his children who were contemporary with him, throughout all generations. (*JD* 2:139.)
>
> . . . It is His [God's] right, it is His prerogative to communicate with the human family . . . [He] has a right to dictate, has a right

to make known His will, has a right to communicate with whom He will and control matters as He sees proper . . . It belongs to Him by right. (*JD* 23:260.)

Personal revelation is limited to your stewardship. President Wilford Woodruff has clarified this limitation:

There is an appointed way . . . by which revelation from the Lord for the government of his church is received. There is but one man on earth, at a time, who holds this power. But every individual member has the privilege of receiving revelation from the Lord for his guidance in his own affairs and to testify to him concerning the correctness of public teachings and movements. (*Millennial Star,* 50:307-308.)

There is only one living prophet upon the earth at any one time who has all the keys for a dispensation. Otherwise, confusion would result. This is clearly set forth by the Prophet Joseph Smith:

I will inform you that it is contrary to the economy of God for any member of the Church, or anyone, to receive instructions for those in authority, higher than themselves; therefore you will see the impropriety of giving heed to them; but if any person have a vision or a visitation from a heavenly messenger, it must be for his own instruction; for the fundamental principles, government, and doctrine of the Church are vested in the keys of the kingdom. (*DHC* 1:338.)

This means that the Lord will not give instruction to a lay member informing his bishop how he should run the affairs of the ward, and he will not advise a bishop on how the stake president should handle a certain situation. If you feel that you have received such information, and you feel obliged to insist upon its acceptance by others in higher echelons, you'd better question the source.

Kinds of Direct Revelation

Direct revelation can occur in a number of ways. We will consider the following:

Visitations	Ideas
Audible voice	Feelings
Still small voice	Sacred instruments

Visions   Impressions
Dreams

Visitations. There are three basic types of immortal beings who may communicate with us: unembodied (spirits), disembodied (spirits), and reembodied (resurrected beings). In addition, visitations by translated beings and even by members of Deity may also be experienced, as we are prepared to receive them and as there is a legitimate need.

The scriptures are full of accounts of personal visitations. A complete listing of recorded accounts would require many pages. One significant account is that of the three-hour visitation of Jesus Christ with the brother of Jared as related in the book of Ether in the Book of Mormon. (Ether 3:6-13.) Jesus could not withhold himself from his presence because of this early prophet's faith. (Ether 3:19-20.)

Moses "saw God face to face, and he talked with him. . . ." (Moses 1:2; *see also* Moses 1:31.)

The Angel Gabriel appeared to Zacharias in the temple. (Luke 1:11-20.)

Joseph Smith was visited by the Father and the Son. (Joseph Smith—History 1:17.)

At the dedication of the Kirtland Temple, some people saw angels. A week later Joseph Smith and Oliver Cowdery saw the Son as well as Moses, Elias, and Elijah. (D&C 110:14-16.)

The signers of the Declaration of Independence appeared to President Wilford Woodruff. (*JD* 19:229.)

The Savior appeared to Lorenzo Snow in the Salt Lake Temple with very special instruction. The full account is included in the last chapter of this book.

A choir of angels was seen at the dedication of the Salt Lake Temple by June Fullmer Andrew, an eight-year-old boy:

> After the dedicatory prayer I beheld a beautiful choir dressed in dazzling white, singing hosannas to the Lord as they marched along the parapet of the temple.
>
> I turned to my parents and exclaimed to them how lovely the choir looked and how beautiful was their singing, for I was thrilled beyond measure. My parents told me the choir was not up there and were not singing, and they pointed out to me there was no

room on the platform and that the parapet was not wide enough for people to march along it, so I was just imagining I saw them. I felt so squelched that I did not mention the incident again for many years, but I knew I had not been imagining.

Many years later, when I was about forty years old, the authorities of the Church invited the High Priest and Seventy quorums and their wives of the Mount Ogden Stake to visit the Temple. The President of the Temple took us on a tour from the bottom to the top . . . He opened an east window near the top where we could view the parapet and showed us where the platform had been built and the dedicatory services had been held. I realized then that the choir I had seen and heard could not have been the Tabernacle Choir.

After the tour we were assembled . . . for a testimony meeting. An Ogden lady, fifteen years my senior, arose to her feet and bore her testimony. She related being at the dedication of the Temple and explained how she had been thrilled with an angel choir which sang and marched about the parapet of the Temple, just as I had seen and heard them.

When she finished I arose and confirmed what she had related as being true since I had experienced the same vision and acceptance of the Temple of the Lord. (Mary Ethel Bean Andrew, *Thru The Years*, comp. June Andrew Babbel and Arlene Andrew Walsh [Arlington, Va.: Ethel Bean Andrew, 1972], pp. 247-48.)

Visits by angels render some valuable insights. Parley P. Pratt describes angels' interaction with mortals:

. . . Their business is also to
—comfort and instruct individual members of the Church of the Saints;
—heal them by the laying on of hands in the name of Jesus Christ or tell them what means to use to get well;
—to teach them good things;
—to warn them of approaching danger, or
—to deliver them from prison or from death.

These blessings have always been enjoyed by the people or Church of the Saints, whenever such Church has existed on our planet. They are not peculiar to one dispensation more than another. (*Key to Theology*, p. 112.)

In the Book of Mormon, Moroni talks about the ministering of angels:

... angels [have not] ceased to minister unto the children of men.

For ... they are subject unto him [Christ], to minister according to the word of his command, showing themselves unto them of strong faith and a firm mind in every form of godliness. (Moroni 7:29-30.)

Elder John A. Widtsoe offers the following explanation:

Many other intelligent beings superior to us, no doubt take part in the work of man on earth. There are angels and spirits who no doubt have assigned to them the care of the men and women who walk upon the earth. Man is not alone; he walks in the midst of such heavenly company, from whom he may expect help if he seeks it strongly. (*A Rational Theology*, p. 64.)

When John the Baptist restored the Aaronic Priesthood in 1829, he promised the ministering of angels:

Upon you my fellow servants, in the name of Messiah I confer the Priesthood of Aaron, which holds the keys of the ministering of angels. . . . (D&C 13.)

Commenting on this glorious event, President Wilford Woodruff said that he had never enjoyed more the ministering of angels as an apostle or as the prophet than he did when he first received the Aaronic Priesthood.

When the Prophet Joseph Smith organized the Relief Society in 1842, he promised the sisters, ". . . if you live up to your privileges, the angels cannot be restricted from being your associates. Females, if they are pure and innocent, can come in the presence of God . . ." (*DHC* 4:605.)

Sisters, do you realize what he said? This is a glorious opportunity open to all women.

Audible Voice. When an audible voice is the method of revelation, the divine messenger is not seen, but either the physical or the spiritual senses hear a message.

The Lord spoke to Moses. (Exodus 25:1; *see also* Moses 1:25.)

Jehovah spoke to Abraham. (Abraham 1:16.)

The Lord called Samuel in the temple. (1 Samuel 3:4-14.)

The Lord spoke to Nephi and taught him. (Helaman 10:3-12.)

The Lord spoke to Joseph Smith many times and appeared to him on occasion after the First Visit in the Sacred Grove.

Many accounts that bear witness of an audible voice communication can be found in current and past personal journals.

At the baptism of Jesus there came "a voice from heaven. . . ." (Matthew 3:17.)

When Lehi and Nephi were in prison, the Lamanites were rebuked by "a voice as if it were above the cloud of darkness . . ." (Helaman 5:29-32; *see also* Helaman 5:30, 46; 1 Nephi 17:45; Psalm 104:7; Revelation 14:2; D&C 133:22.)

On the American continent at the time of the great destruction, "there was a voice heard among all the inhabitants of the earth . . ." (3 Nephi 9:1; *see also* entire chapter.)

A great multitude of people "heard a voice as if it came out of heaven. . . ." (3 Nephi 11:3.) This voice — the voice of the Eternal Father — preceded the appearance of the resurrected Lord Jesus Christ.

Still, Small Voice. Here we have spirit-to-spirit communication. Joseph Smith explains that knowledge is revealed "to our spirits precisely as though we had no bodies at all . . ." (*DHC* 6:312.)

Paul explained the same thing to the Romans: "The Spirit itself beareth witness with our spirit. . . ." (Romans 8:16.)

Wilford Woodruff emphasizes the great importance of the "still, small voice" of the Holy Ghost:

> . . . How many of you have had the Spirit of God whisper unto you — the still small voice? . . . I have been blessed at times with certain gifts and graces, certain revelations and ministrations; but with them all I have never found anything that I could place more dependency upon than the still small voice of the Holy Ghost. (*JD* 21:195-96.)

Nephi and his brothers were acquainted with the "still, small voice," but, he told Laman and Lemuel, "ye were past feeling, that ye could not feel his words. . . ." (1 Nephi 17:45.)

Enos explains it in this manner: ". . . while I was thus struggling in the spirit, . . . the voice of the Lord came into my mind again, saying . . . ." (Enos 1:10.)

Visions. Revelation through visions is the viewing of people or events as perceived through our spiritual eyes. Joseph Smith explains that "by the power of the Spirit our eyes were opened and our understandings were enlightened, so as to see and understand the things of God. The veil was taken from our minds, and the eyes of our understanding were opened." (D&C 76:12; 110:1.)

Both ancient and modern scriptures and historical records abound with many accounts of visions. Examples in modern times would include the following.

Joseph Smith and Sidney Rigdon had a vision of the degrees of glory, recorded in section 76 of the Doctrine and Covenants.

President Wilford Woodruff had a vision, as well as divine suggestions, before issuing the Manifesto.

> I saw by the inspiration of Almighty God what lay before this people, and I knew that something had to be done to ward off the blow that I saw impending . . . But . . . I should have seen all this [happen] had not Almighty God commanded me to do what I did. (G. Homer Durham, comp., *The Discourses of Wilford Woodruff* [Salt Lake City: Bookcraft, Inc., 1946], pp. 217-18.)

President Joseph F. Smith's "Vision of the Redemption of the Dead" is now included in the Doctrine and Covenants as section 138.

Visions are not limited to prophets or those in positions of authority. A special vision occurred to Sister Rebecca Bean, who with her husband, Brother Willard Bean, served a mission in Palmyra, New York, from 1915 to 1940. They were instrumental in the purchase by the Church of the Hill Cumorah and its replanting of 65,000 trees. Everyone who came east wanted to see the Joseph Smith home and the Hill Cumorah, and they all stayed to visit, from a few days to several weeks. Sister Bean was responsible for caring for these visitors as well as for her own family. The following is an account given by her at a 1964 Salt Lake City fireside:

> It was a hot summer day and we had a lot of visitors that day. It had been a hard day for me. I had a baby just a year old, and I had carried my baby around on my arm most of the day to get my

work done. It was too warm. Everything had gone against us. We had had lunch for our visitors, and we had had supper at night, and I had put my children to bed. Dr. [James E.] Talmage was there and some missionaries, and we had really had a wonderful evening talking together. They all seemed tired and I took them upstairs and showed them where they could sleep, and I came down and thought, *Well, I'll pick up a few things and make things easier for in the morning.*

But I was so weary and so tired that I was crying as I went straightening things around a little. Everybody was in bed and asleep but me. I looked at the clock and it was eleven o'clock. I said, "I'd better call it a day." I went into my room and . . . it was peaceful and quiet. I got ready for bed, and I was crying a little. I said my prayers and I got into bed and I was crying on my pillow. And then this dream or vision came to me.

I thought it was another day. It had been a wonderful morning. I had prepared breakfast for my visitors, and my children were happily playing around, and I had done my work and cared for the baby, and he was contented and happy. I prepared lunch, and I called my visitors in to lunch and we were all seated around the table, my little baby in the high chair. Everything was peaceful and wonderfully sweet. There was a knock at the front door, and there was a very handsome young man standing there. I just took it for granted that he was another new missionary come to see us, and I said, "You're here just in time for lunch. Come with me."

As I walked through the little hall into the dining room, I noticed he laid some pamphlets down on the table there. I introduced him around, and then I said, "Now you sit right here by Dr. Talmage, and I'll set a place for you." I thought he was strange to all of us, and yet he and Dr. Talmage seemed so happy to see each other, and they talked about such wonderful things while we were eating. Some of them we could hardly understand. But the spirit that was there in the meal was so peaceful and nice, and everyone seemed so happy to be together. After the meal was over, Dr. Talmage said to the missionaries, "Now let's go outside and just linger here and enjoy the spirit of this wonderful place, because we'll soon have to leave." I put my baby to bed, and the other little ones went out to play, and then I was alone with this young man.

He thanked me for having him to dinner, and told me how much it meant for him to be there, and he told me he thought that the children were so sweet and well trained, and I felt happy about that, and then we walked in the hall together. He said, "I have far to go, so I must be on my way." Then I turned from him just a moment to pick up these little pamphlets that he had laid on the table, and when I turned back to him it was the Savior who stood before me, and he was in his glory. And I could not tell you the love and sweetness that he had in his face and in his eyes. Lovingly, he laid his hands on my shoulders, and he looked down into my face with the kindest face that I have ever seen, and this is what he said to me: "Sister Bean, this day hasn't been too hard for you, has it?" And I said, "Oh no, I have been so happy in my work and everything has gone on so well." Then he said, "I promise you if you will go about your work as you have done it this day you will be equal to it. Oh, remember these missionaries represent me on this earth, and all that you do unto them you do unto me."

And then I remember I was crying as we walked through the hall onto the porch, and he repeated the same thing: "These missionaries represent me on earth, and all that you do unto them you do unto me." And then he started upwards. The roof of the porch was no obstruction for him to go through, nor for me to see through. He went upward and upward and upward, and I wondered and wondered how I could see him so far away. And then all at once he disappeared, and I was crying on my pillow like I was when I went to bed.

I bear humble testimony to you that never again was there any frustration in my soul. Never again did too many missionaries come that I couldn't find beds for them to sleep or enough food to give them, and the great love I had for missionaries even then became greater after what the Savior had said to me. And how I wish that every missionary that went out in the world could feel that his love and his guidance is only a prayer away. They teach his gospel, and how much they mean to Him. (Rebecca Rosetta Peterson Bean, recorded talk delivered at a Salt Lake City fireside, fall 1964.)

Dreams. Dreams are like visions, except that the physical body is asleep.

Jacob had a dream. (Genesis 28:12.)

Joseph angered his brothers when he related his dreams. As a result he was sold into Egypt. (Genesis 37:5-11, 28.)

As a baby, Jesus' life was spared when Joseph was warned in a dream to take him and his mother into Egypt. Joseph was also instructed in a dream when to return to his homeland. (Matthew 2:13, 22.)

Wilford Woodruff explains the value of dreams:

We may have dreams about things of great importance, and dreams of no importance at all . . . there are a great many things

taught us in dreams that are true, and if a man has the spirit of
God he can tell the difference between what is from the Lord and
what is not . . . whenever you have a dream that you feel is from
the Lord, pay attention to it . . .

The Lord does communicate some things of importance to the
children of men by means of visions and dreams as well as by the
records of divine truth. And what is it all for? It is to teach us a
principle. We may never see anything take place exactly as we see
it in a dream or a vision, yet it is intended to teach us a principle.
(JD 22:333.)

Sometimes dreams are so vivid that a person may describe
them as a vision. Elder Melvin J. Ballard's visit with the Savior in
the Salt Lake Temple is a good example. (*Melvin J. Ballard, Crusader for Righteousness* [Salt Lake City: Bookcraft, Inc., 1966],
pp. 138-39.)

Ideas. Sometimes you may receive a "flash" idea, an understanding of an entire concept without any words to express it. You
have to ponder it to put it into words. At other times there may be
sentences, phrases, or words formed in your mind. Enos gives us
an example of a specific message. (Enos 1:10.)

Unless you pay attention to these words or messages, they will
not be expanded. Note the reaction of Enos to his experience.
(Enos 1:11-12.)

Concerning the revelation of ideas, the Prophet Joseph Smith
offered counsel that can help us grow into this principle:

A person may profit by noticing the first intimation of the spirit of
revelation; for instance, when you feel pure intelligence flowing into
you, it may give you sudden strokes of ideas, so that by noticing it
you may find it fulfilled the same day or soon; (i.e.) those things that
were presented unto your minds by the Spirit of God will come to
pass; and thus by learning the spirit of God and understanding it you
may grow into the principle of revelation, until you become perfect
in Christ Jesus. (*DHC* 3:381.)

Feelings. Our minds become more receptive to instruction from
the Lord when our hearts are touched by the Spirit. Such feelings
have been described as "warm," "expanding," "swelling," "quickening," "burning."

Once you have felt the sweetness of the Spirit and experienced
its effect upon your body, it will be easier to identify the next time.

It is a humble, grateful feeling that can bring tears to your eyes and expand your hearts with joy.

But you must be receptive. A closed mind or negative feelings can block the Spirit of the Lord from your life. Remember the first key — God works through positive feelings. He can only help you when you are willing to be helped. Hence the emphasis throughout the scriptures on love and the mention of a broken heart and contrite spirit as being essential. (D&C 64:22; 136:33.)

We hear people say, "I am brokenhearted about that," meaning they are overwhelmed with grief. Is this the meaning in the scriptures? No. A broken heart is a humble, repentant heart, not a closed heart or a hard heart as mentioned so often in the Book of Mormon as a source of trouble. A broken heart is softened and opened up so the Spirit, with its healing power, can be absorbed. When you read "broken heart," think "open heart."

A contrite spirit is a humble, teachable spirit. To attain this, our spirits must be humble and teachable and our hearts must be open to receive the Spirit of the Lord. Without our receptiveness, the Lord cannot help us without violating our agency.

The Spirit is not imposed upon us but is made available. In order to receive its benefits, we must be receptive to it. Thus we need to recognize how necessary are the feelings of harmony and peace within our spirits. These enable us to become attuned to the powers of heaven. Thus are we able to receive and profit from personal divine revelation in our lives.

Sacred Instruments. Usually, sacred instruments are not involved in personal revelation. But they have been used and would include the following:

The Urim and Thummim, mentioned in all four standard works of the Church. (See the Bible dictionary and topical guide in the Holy Bible, published by The Church of Jesus Christ of Latter-day Saints, 1979.)

The Liahona or divine compass, mentioned in the Book of Mormon. (Alma 37:38, 40-41, 45.)

Impressions. An impression is a flash of understanding. Often one's feelings may be involved, strongly indicating an action to be taken.

A newly appointed stake president asked President Harold B. Lee how he could be sure he was leading the people of his stake correctly. President Lee told him to follow his own impressions. As long as all went well, and the man had a good feeling about what he was doing, he was right. But if he were not to feel good about a decision or action, he should stop and carefully analyze it before he continued. (*Relief Society Courses of Study*, 1974-75 [Salt Lake City: The Church of Jesus Christ of Latter-day Saints, 1974], p. 27. Hereinafter referred to as *Relief Society Courses of Study*.)

Kinds of Indirect Revelation

Indirect revelation can come through people, circumstances, or things outside yourself. Many flashes of inspiration are the result of something you see or hear, and may serve as a catalyst to open your mind to new concepts.

When your attention is set "so much upon the things of this world . . ." (D&C 121:35) or you are engrossed in your troubles and obligations, you may not be sufficiently attuned to receive direct revelation. Hence the Lord employs some indirect means to get your attention. It can be exciting to become aware of how the Lord helps us in this manner.

In such cases you do not receive revelation directly from heavenly messengers, but you are guided indirectly to certain principles, conclusions, or awareness:

Through people. Often, through the testimony, experience, or counsel of others, we are stimulated with ideas or feelings that will help our lives.

Through circumstances. Here everything works out harmoniously for everyone involved. Sometimes through a fascinating sequence of events we are led to do what is best for us. "And we know that all things work together for good to them that love God. . . ." (Romans 8:28.)

Through things. Often what we see or hear can be used to stimulate needed ideas or feelings. For instance, we may see a sunset and be filled with love and gratitude and humility. Then, as our feelings are closer to the surface than usual, we become more receptive to the Spirit of the Lord. It is then that an answer we have been seeking or an idea may come to us. We may hear something or read something that may open our minds to inspired ideas.

A good example of indirect revelation is the experience that inspired Robert Bruce to gain independence for Scotland after repeated failures.

Robert Bruce was a gallant Scottish king who spent most of his life trying to free his country from English rule. After a dismal attempt, Bruce was hiding from his enemies, lying on a bed in a wretched hut. On the roof above him, Bruce saw a spider swinging by one of its web threads, trying to move from one beam to another.

It tried six times and failed. Bruce realized that he had fought the same number of battles in vain against the English. He decided that if the spider tried a seventh time and succeeded, he also would try again. The spider's seventh attempt was successful. Bruce took heart, went forth to victory, and freed Scotland. (World Book Encyclopedia, 19 vols. [Chicago: Field Enterprises Educational Corp., 1963], 2:358.)

Another important lesson to be learned by us from this example, and many others that might be considered, is that a person never really fails until he stops trying.

Developing Greater Attunement

> The first of the fundamental principles by which man may confer with God, is that man must show his desire to receive, by asking for help . . . Whatever a man gains from the surrounding wisdom is initiated either by a petition or by a receptive attitude which is equivalent to a request. Unless a man asks, he is in no condition to receive, and ordinarily nothing is given him. (*A Rational Theology*, p. 66.)

You have to want it—have a burning desire—"with real intent." (Moroni 10:4.)

You have to ask for it. ". . . Ye have not, because ye ask not." (James 4:2.)

You have to build enough momentum of the Spirit to block out whatever can divert your attention, enough to quicken your perception so you can become aware of and understand the whisperings of the Spirit.

Such momentum can be brought about in different ways: by study . . . (2 Nephi 32:3; D&C 88:118) by pondering . . . by fervent prayer . . . by expressing gratitude . . . by asking for help and then listening for answers . . . by noticing ideas that come into your mind about a subject. (DHC 6:312.)

At first it may be difficult to block from your thoughts the many problems and concerns of your life. At this you have to practice. This is one reason for reading the scriptures, to put your attention to something that will increase your ability to receive the Spirit and block your negative thinking.

So you have a time for building momentum — studying, pondering, praying.

You also have an asking time — expressing gratitude and love to the Lord, specifying the problem, and asking for a solution.

And you have a listening time — an attitude of alert expectancy. You can be doing other things that do not require too much concentration, but you will also try to be filled — quickened — with the Spirit.

When an impression comes to your mind, write it down. Then mull it over to see how it feels. If it seems good or there is a feeling of rightness about it, or if you feel happy or thrilled or relieved or at peace, then you will know it is from the Lord. But if you want to argue about or criticize it or if you feel confused, upset, troubled, or negative, then question the source of the idea. It may be from the adversary.

This process was explained to Oliver Cowdery by the Lord: "I will tell you in your mind and in your heart, by the Holy Ghost . . . Now, behold, this is the spirit of revelation." (D&C 8:2-3.)

These are two ways the Holy Ghost works with us. Sometimes an idea will occur to you. Other times you will have an impression, or a wonderful feeling in your heart. If you get an idea, see how it feels. If you get a feeling, watch for ideas to supplement it. When you know in your mind and in your heart, you will have a double witness.

Discerning Between Truth and Error

We must learn to recognize genuine versus counterfeit revelation. This applies to our own as well as that of others. If we are to "Prove all things; hold fast that which is good," (1 Thessalonians 5:21) we need a criterion for proving. We will consider two methods.

The prophet Mormon gave us an unmistakable standard by which we may judge whether a matter is of God or not.

> Every thing which inviteth and enticeth to do good, and to love God, and to serve him, is inspired of God.
>
> Wherefore, . . . take heed . . . that ye do not judge that which is evil to be of God, or that which is good and of God to be of the devil.
>
> For . . . the Spirit of Christ is given to every man, that he may know good from evil; wherefore, I show unto you the way to judge; for every thing which inviteth to do good, and to persuade to believe in Christ, is sent forth by the power and gift of Christ: wherefore ye may know with a perfect knowledge it is of God.
>
> But whatsoever thing persuadeth men to do evil, and believe not in Christ, and deny him, and serve not God, then ye may know with a perfect knowledge it is of the devil; for after this manner doth the devil work, for he persuadeth no man to do good, no, not one; neither do his angels; neither do they who subject themselves unto him.
>
> And now . . . seeing that ye know the light by which ye may judge, which light is the light of Christ, see that ye do not judge wrongfully; for with that same judgment which ye judge ye shall also be judged. (Moroni 7:14, 16-18.)

How you feel is the key for one who has developed effective attunement. If you are on the Lord's side of the line, you will experience peace, joy, and harmony. There will be no feeling of contention, confusion, or belligerence. You will feel a oneness with all that is wholesome and pure. Any contrary feelings testify that it is not of God or that your testimony and attunement are not yet sufficiently strong.

Resolving Areas of Apparent Conflict

Contention is not of God. Even if we are right in our premise, we are wrong if our approach is one of argument or aggression. After the Lord instructed Nephi on the manner of baptism, he said:

> And there shall be no disputations among you . . . concerning the points of my doctrine.
>   For . . . he that hath the spirit of contention is not of me, but is of the devil, who is the father of contention, And he stirreth up the hearts of men to contend with anger, one with another.
>   Behold, this is not my doctrine, to stir up the hearts of men with anger . . . But this is my doctrine, that such things should be done away. (3 Nephi 11:28-30.)

We should, at all costs, avoid hasty judgments, caustic reproof, and other feelings, thoughts, or actions not in harmony with standards set by the Lord. Contention and the exercise of unrighteous dominion can result in the withdrawal of divine power from the giver as well as the receiver.

We cannot have attunement with the Spirit when we are feeling discord. We need to establish our priorities. Which is more important, to prove you are right or to have the Spirit of the Lord? To get your own way or to have the Spirit of the Lord? To show your superior knowledge or to have the Spirit of the Lord?

Discord prevents attunement. It breaks the link that can bring understanding to your mind and comfort and peace to your heart.

Any time strong, negative feelings are involved, you can discount your ideas or another person's ideas as being subject to serious question.

Instead of thinking in terms of conflict, think in terms of how to resolve differences harmoniously. The following suggestions may be helpful.

1. There are no genuine conflicts with truth, but there can be misunderstanding. This frequently occurs because of our lack of knowledge or experience. Thus there may be concepts that seem wrong to us because of our faulty perception of their relationship to existing principles with which we are already familiar.

When knowledgeable people disagree, you may safely assume that they are seeing the matter from different points of perspective.

The verse about the six blind men of Hindustan, who each gave their best judgment of an elephant, based upon their experience, applies here.

One declared, after feeling the elephant's tail, that he was quite like a rope. A second one protested and, having touched the elephant's trunk, said the elephant was like a snake. The third member bumped against the elephant's tusk and concluded that this animal was like a spear. The elephant began flapping his ears and the next man assured the group that what they were exploring was a fan. As the fifth man wrapped his arms around the elephant's leg and tried to lift it, he was fully convinced that this was a tree. The last man came in contact with the elephant's side and judged that it must be a wall.

It really was an elephant. Yet each man had a valid reason for his conclusion, based upon his limited experience. No amount of conflict and arguing could possibly settle the matter correctly and establish the truth. No wonder the Savior counseled us to "Judge not, that ye be not judged." (Matthew 7:1.)

2. Truth has many levels. Our understanding may expand as our spirituality increases.

There are eternal principles that are necessary for our salvation. They apply to all men, all times. There are other truths that may have specific application to a certain time and place and no application to a later time, such as Noah building the ark and the pioneers crossing the plains.

Then there are truths which are fundamental but which must be adapted to meet changing circumstances. The underlying principle may be the same, but the application that is needed or appropriate at one level is not necessarily needed or appropriate at another. Yet it remains essential in that area or degree of understanding to which it applies. For example:

Principle: We should be careful when crossing the street. (This is true at all levels, but the application of this principle differs accordingly.)

Level	*Truth*
Two-year-old child	Thou shalt not cross the street.

Five-year-old child	Thou shalt stop and look both ways before crossing the street.
Adult	No limitations.

President George Q. Cannon discoursed on this subject and advised his listeners that many revelations are not suited to present conditions.

> A great many people fall into error very frequently by quoting and seeking to apply to present conditions revelations which were given to the Church in early days and which were especially adapted to the circumstances then existing. Of course, it is appropriate to quote from the revelations concerning principles; but in many instances the revelations that are contained in the Book of Doctrine and Covenants are not . . . suited to the circumstances and conditions in which we are placed. They were given to the Church at a time when just such revelations were required.
> . . . When, however, it comes to the revelations concerning principle, then those revelations are unalterable and they will stand as long as heaven and earth will endure, because they are true. (George Q. Cannon, *Gospel Truth*, 2 Vols., Jerreld L. Newquist, ed. [Salt Lake City; Deseret Book Co., 1974], 1:323-24. Hereinafter referred to as *Gospel Truth*.)

3. Truth has different categories.

An example of apparent conflict occurs in relation to the foundation of the Church. Matthew says the rock of revelation is the foundation. (Matthew 16:17-18.) Paul declares that Jesus Christ is the foundation. (1 Corinthians 3:11.)

Both statements are true. They are in different categories and cannot be compared in like manner. Who would argue about a potato versus a banana? One is a vegetable, one is a fruit. Or who would argue about the merits of a sunset versus a watermelon? Which has greater value? The two categories cannot be compared.

Jesus Christ = the foundation of the organization of the Church. This refers to people.

Revelation = the foundation principle of the everlasting gospel.

Other principles might include agency and eternal progression.

4. The validity of a revelation cannot be proven, necessarily, by existing scriptures. Elder Franklin D. Richards explained this difficulty.

> The Lord has told us in a revelation which he gave through the Prophet Joseph, January 19, 1841: "I deign to reveal unto my church things which have been kept hid from before the foundation of the world, things that pertain to the dispensation of the fulness of times
>
> I would like to know where you will find scriptures to prove things by which have never before been revealed . . . and from henceforth we may expect more and more of the word of the Lord giving us instructions which are nowhere written in the old Scriptures. If we feel ourselves, or teach the Saints of the people generally, that we are only to believe that which can be proved from the Scriptures, we shall never know much of the Lord ourselves, nor be able to teach the children of men to any very considerable extent. (*Millennial Star*, 16:534.)

In conclusion, inspiration and revelation can be received from the Lord by each individual member of the Church for his personal guidance as fast as he is able to accept and profit by it. (*Relief Society Courses of Study*, 1974-75, p. 27.)

President George Q. Cannon summarized some of the blessings we may receive through establishing personal revelation in our lives:

> . . . all who seek him [God] will receive his blessing. He will give certainty, he will remove doubt the misapprehension, and give light and enable all such to comprehend and see as far as necessary that which is good for them; he will lead them on step by step, until they reach his presence if they will obey his commandments. They will not have to do this in darkness or in doubt, they will not have to throw aside or surrender their judgment, but he will give unto them his mind and will in such plainness that they will know and comprehend for themselves, although they may be tempted and tried and afflicted. (*JD* 22:239; 11:240-41.)

> For whosoever receiveth, to him shall be given, and he shall have more abundance; but whosoever continueth not to receive, from him shall be taken away even that he hath. (Matthew 13:10-11, JST.)

. . . every man, every set of men, and every people will be held responsible in time and eternity, for the use they have made of the gifts, blessings, and promises which have been given unto them.
(Wilford Woodruff, *JD* 18:187.)

Activating Priesthood Power

We are living in the most wonderful period of this earth's history, the dispensation of the fulness of times. The fathers from Adam to Noah, the patriarchs from Seth and Abraham to the time of Moses, and the many prophets since that time throughout gospel dispensations in various parts of the world have looked longingly for the very time in which we are living. The midnight hour before Christ's coming in power and glory is drawing to a rapid close. His second coming is very near.

In preparation for this time, the Lord declared through the prophet Joel,

I will pour out my spirit upon all flesh; and your sons and your daughters shall prophesy, your old men shall dream dreams, your young men shall see visions:

And also upon the servants and upon the handmaids in those days will I pour out my spirit. (Joel 2:28-29; see also Acts 2:17-18.)

The real significance of this prophecy is emphasized by the fact that the Prophet Joseph Smith, in his first instruction from the angel Moroni in 1823, records that the angel quoted this prophecy: "He [Moroni] said that this was not yet fulfilled, but was soon to be." (Joseph Smith—History 1:41.)

In this prophecy, to which the angel Moroni referred, the pouring out of the Lord's Spirit upon all flesh refers primarily to the world as a whole. The reference to servants and hand-maidens which is a common expression in the restored Church of Jesus Christ seems to have more direct application to the entire membership of the Church—men and women as well as children.

It is happening right now before our very eyes. Anyone who makes even a cursory review of what has taken place, particularly in the Christian world, since the restoration of the gospel, will notice that faith has increased, as the Lord indicated it would in his preface to the Book of Commandments. (D&C 1:21.) He will likewise observe that many of the fruits of the Spirit, which are to be poured out upon those who have such faith in Jesus Christ, are being made manifest as never before.

But this could not commence until the gospel of Jesus Christ was restored in its fulness so that it could fulfill its leavening role for all of Christianity and for the entire world. In this connection you may recall that the Savior said in a parable, "The kingdom of heaven is like unto leaven, which a woman took, and hid in three measures of meal, till the whole was leavened." (Matthew 13:33; see also Luke 13:21.)

Our purpose, and never let us forget it, is to be the leaven in the loaf, not the loaf itself. We are to be the instrument through which mankind may become aware of additional divine principles. We are to declare and manifest the truth in and through our lives so that others may gradually accept more and more truth.

President George Q. Cannon has commented upon this leavening effect of the gospel in these words: "It is very remarkable that the people of Christendom are gradually adopting the truths which the Prophet Joseph was inspired of the Lord to teach . . . There is scarcely one of these that is not believed in now in some form by thousands of people outside of this Church . . . They believe, in a certain way, the principles. And those which they do not believe are gradually working their way into notice and favor." (*Gospel Truth*, 2:54.)

We need, as never before, to let our light so shine before men, that they, seeing our good works, will glorify our Father in Heaven. (Matthew 5:16.) Be grateful that these exciting things are happening now and that we can not only be a vital part of them, but also know that we are expected to take the lead in bringing them about.

Discerning the Critical Need

Let us first consider some incisive remarks by President John Taylor.

> Are we magnifying our calling? No, we are not! . . . It needs the Spirit of the Living God breathed into it . . .
>
> We are told that "many will say to me in that day, Lord, Lord, have we not prophesied in Thy name and in Thy name have cast out devils, and in Thy name done many wonderful works?" Yet to all such he will say, "Depart from me, ye that work iniquity." You say that means the outsiders? No, it does not . . . This means you, Latter-day Saints, who heal the sick, cast out devils and do many wonderful things in the name of Jesus . . .
>
> Hear it, ye Latter-day Saints! Hear it, ye Seventies and ye High Priests! Whatsoever a man soweth that shall he reap . . . You have the Priesthood, and if you do not magnify the priesthood, God will require it at your hands . . .
>
> Now hear it, for as sure as God lives it will be so . . . If you aim at a celestial glory you must have a celestial spirit and be governed by it. (*JD*, 20:120.)

Sometimes it is profitable for us to consider such counsel and to take a personal inventory to determine just where we stand. Unless we measure up to the Lord's invitation and expectations, we shall find that the parable of those who were invited to the king's wedding feast for his son, and who either did not show up or who did not have a proper wedding garment, may just recount our own sad condition in that glorious day of his coming. (Matthew 22:2-14.)

As we examine the need for activating priesthood power, keep in mind that the Lord informed us that the power of the priesthood depends upon personal righteousness. (D&C 121:36.) Lacking such righteousness, that person's priesthood, for the moment, at least, is powerless.

Perhaps the best example is related by Elder Parley P. Pratt. He recounts the Prophet Joseph Smith's stern rebuke, "while in the Spirit," after the famous day of healing in 1839.

> Brother Joseph while in the spirit, rebuked the Elders who would continue to lay hands on the sick from day to day without the power to heal them. Said he: "It is time that such things ended. Let the elders either obtain the power of God to heal the sick, or let them cease to minister the forms without the power!" (Parley P. Pratt, *Autobiography of Parley Parker Pratt*, 3rd ed., Parley P. Pratt, ed. [Salt Lake City: Deseret Book Co., 1938], pp. 293-94.)

As mentioned earlier, the Prophet Joseph identified personal righteousness as the key to power. Elder Moses Thatcher explained in greater detail the necessity and importance of such priesthood power:

> . . . if we, Latter-day Saints, will live near unto him, he will be near unto us. And instead of having to call in physicians to minister to the members of our families when sickness makes its appearance, the power of God will be upon us in such rich abundance as to enable us to rebuke it from our dwellings, and to invoke the blessings of health to attend us and ours, which was the case years ago in the primeval days of the Church. If we have lost any of these blessings it is not through any fault in the Lord, or that there is less power and efficacy in the priesthood we bear, but rather in our own lack of faith in the promises made to the faithful. (*JD*, 20:195.)

Key to Righteous Stewardship

Priesthood is a divinely delegated stewardship. It is a granting of power and authority to serve as a priest of the Most High God. Thus it becomes imperative that we learn what qualities fashion a righteous stewardship and apply them to our lives. These are plainly set forth in the Doctrine and Covenants. Note the conditions:

. . . the rights of the priesthood are inseparably connected with the powers of heaven, and . . . the powers of heaven cannot be controlled nor handled only upon the principles of righteousness.

That they may be conferred upon us, it is true; but when we undertake to cover our sins, or to gratify our pride, our vain ambition, or to exercise control or dominion or compulsion upon the souls of the children of men, in any degree of unrighteousness, behold, the heavens withdraw themselves; the Spirit of the Lord is grieved; and when it is withdrawn, Amen to the priesthood or the authority of that man. (D&C 121:36-37.)

Failure to follow this counsel is a major cause of disagreements, disputes, contentions, broken homes and ruined lives. It is also the primary reason why many who have received the priesthood seem to give little evidence of the powers of heaven being made manifest in their use of the priesthood.

Since we are considering ways to activate priesthood power, we must be aware that the rights, which include administering the ordinances and handling the affairs of the Kingdom, are inseparably connected with the powers of heaven — the source of priesthood power — and that the powers of heaven can only be exercised upon the principles of righteousness. As the Lord continues,

. . . there are many called [to receive the priesthood], But few are chosen [to receive and exercise the power]. And why are they not chosen?

Because their hearts are set so much upon the things of this world, And aspire to the honors of men . . .

Then the conditions necessary to receive priesthood power are again emphasized:

No power or influence can or ought to be maintained by virtue of the priesthood, only by persuasion, by long-suffering, by gentleness and meekness, and by love unfeigned;

By kindness and pure knowledge. . . . (D&C 121:41-42.)

In other words, stay on the Lord's side of the line. This is where the power is available to us, this is where the blessings are received. We cannot exercise our priesthood righteously while we harbor negative feelings.

Elder John A. Widtsoe explained with rare sensitivity the righteous use of this stewardship as applied within the family:

By divine fiat the priesthood is conferred upon man. This means that organization must prevail in the family, the ultimate unit of the Church. The husband, the priesthood bearer, presides (not rules) over the family. The priesthood conferred upon him is intended for the blessing of the whole family. Every member shares in the gift bestowed, but under a proper organization. No man who understands the gospel believes he is greater than his wife or more beloved of the Lord because he holds the priesthood, but rather he is under the responsibility of speaking and acting for the family in official matters. It is a protection to the woman, who, because of her motherhood, is under a large physical and spiritual obligation. Motherhood is an eternal part of the priesthood. (*Evidences and Reconciliations*, 3 Vol., comp. G. Homer Durham [Salt Lake City: Bookcraft, Inc., 1960], p. 244.)

Some priesthood holders like to refer to a part of section 121 of the Doctrine and Covenants which relates to reproof. Such reproof is conditional. Properly understood it provides a genuine refining influence. Let us examine its privileges and limitations as outlined in verse 43:

Reproving betimes with sharpness, When moved upon by the Holy Ghost . . .

Just be sure you are moved upon by the Holy Ghost and not by irritation or anger or something else. You can tell by what spirit the reproof comes by considering the key that follows the above quotation.

. . . and then showing forth afterwards an increase of love toward him whom thou hast reproved, lest he esteem thee to be his enemy;
That he may know that thy faithfulness is stronger than the cords of death. (D&C 121:43-44.)

We must show forth that love, that kindness, that tenderness, that forgiveness immediately after we have reproved, if we have reproved with the right spirit in the first place, so that the healing power of God can come into that person's life and bring about the divine peace that should be there. Then, and only then, will any kind of reproof be sanctioned by God.

Following this divine counsel is an important key to righteous stewardship through which may operate the powers of heaven.

Applying Divine Counsel

Maintain uplifting thoughts.

> Let thy bowels also be full of charity towards all men, and to
> the household of faith, and let virtue garnish thy thoughts un-
> ceasingly; then shall thy confidence wax strong in the presence
> of God; and the doctrine of the priesthood shall distil upon thy
> soul as the dews from heaven. (D&C 121:45.)

Charity for all people and unceasing virtuous thoughts are
divine requirements to understand and apply the true doctrine of
the priesthood. These are prerequisite to receiving the blessing
that follows, one of the greatest ever promised to righteous men.

> The Holy Ghost shall be thy constant companion, and thy
> scepter an unchanging scepter of righteousness and truth; and thy
> dominion shall be an everlasting dominion, and without compul-
> sory means it shall flow unto thee forever and ever. (D&C 121:46.)

The priesthood should make those who bear it kind, full of
knowledge, honest, and virtuous. The Holy Spirit will be
wherever these qualities exist. And only those who retain the
Spirit are chosen, though many are called. (Hyrum M. Smith
and Janne M. Sjodahl, *Doctrine and Covenants Commentary*
[Salt Lake City: Deseret Book Co., 1950], p. 759.)

Obtain divine direction. When we have been authorized to
speak and act for God, then the least we can do as priesthood
bearers is to accept his counsel in which he reveals another key
to his power, which is so vital to us.

> Seek not to declare my word, but first seek to obtain my word,
> and then shall your tongue be loosed; then, if you desire, you shall
> have my Spirit and my word, yea, the power of God unto the
> convincing of men. (D&C 11:21.)

This embodies the spirit of the oath and covenant of the
priesthood. As his priests we should first learn his mind and will.
Then our functions and our administrations will be clothed with
power, because we will be in complete harmony with the powers
of heaven. If we are to magnify and exercise the priesthood in
righteousness, knowing the mind and will of God before we act
will certainly insure that the requisite power will be present.

Be humble. President Brigham Young adds additional perspective and challenge concerning our right to divine communication and revelation:

> . . . no man shall receive the benefits of the everlasting Priesthood without humbling himself before Him, and giving Him the glory for teaching him, that he may be able to witness to every man of the truth, and not depend upon the words of any individual on the earth, but know for himself, live "by every word that proceedeth out of the mouth of God," love the Lord Jesus Christ and the institutions of His Kingdom, and finally enter into His glory. (*JD*, 2:189.)

Strengthen your faith. The following reference is from the Prophet Joseph Smith's teachings:

> Miracles are the fruits of faith . . .
> . . . Faith comes by hearing the word of God. If a man has not faith enough to do one thing, he may have faith to do another; if he cannot move a mountain, he may heal the sick. Where faith is there will be some of the fruits: all gifts and power which were sent from heaven, were poured out on the heads of those who had faith. (*Choose You This Day,* Melchizedek Priesthood Personal Study Guide 1980-81 [Salt Lake City: The Church of Jesus Christ of Latter-day Saints, 1979], p. 94. Hereinafter referred to as *Choose You This day.*)

This counsel of the Prophet Joseph is amply supported by the Lord himself as he declares:

> For I am God, and mine arm is not shortened; and I will show miracles, signs, and wonders unto all those who believe on my name
> And whoso shall ask it in my name in faith, they shall cast out devils; they shall heal the sick; they shall cause the blind to receive their sight, and the deaf to hear, and the dumb to speak, and the lame to walk. (D&C 35:8-9.)

Judge not wrongfully. The Prophet Moroni provided us with an unmistakable guide for making righteous judgments:

> Every thing which inviteth to do good, and to persuade to believe in Christ, is sent forth by the power and gift of Christ; wherefore ye may know with a perfect knowledge it is of God. . . .
> See that ye do not judge wrongfully; for with that same judgment which ye judge ye shall also be judged. (Moroni 7:16, 18.)

Commenting on this matter, President George Q. Cannon said:

> No one can complain with any good cause if he is recompensed according to his works or if he receives the same measure that he measures to his fellow man . . . Men cannot be held accountable for that which they never knew. God will never consign his creatures to a never-ending misery for not obeying the Gospel of His Son which they never had it taught unto them, and it is as great a fallacy and as great a libel on our God as ever was propagated about any being to make such an assertion . . . God's salvation is not confined to this brief space which we call time, but as He is eternal, so are His mercy, love and compassion eternal towards His creatures. (*Gospel Truth*, 2:92-93.)

Jesus explained this principle to his disciples when they were upset upon finding someone who used his name without authorization.

> And John answered him, saying, Master, we saw one casting out devils in thy name, and he followeth not us: and we forbad him, because he followeth not us.
> But Jesus said, Forbid him not: for there is no man which shall do a miracle in my name, that can lightly speak evil of me. For he that is not against us is on our part. (Mark 9:38-41; Luke 9:49-50.)

Note in the above example that the disciples were judging wrongly those who were not directly affiliated with them.

Achieving Divine Expectations

If we use our divine power properly and make the right decisions, as sons of God should do, we will most assuredly achieve the divine expectations of our Heavenly Father and of Jesus Christ. President Brigham Young expressed this thought in a masterful manner. His counsel and promise are worthy of consideration by all.

> An individual who holds a share in the Priesthood, and continues faithful to his calling, who delights himself continually in doing the things God requires at his hands, and continues through life in the performance of every duty, will secure to himself not only the privilege of receiving, but the knowledge how to receive the things of God, that he may know the mind of God continually; and he will be enabled to discern between right and wrong, between the

things of God and the things that are not of God. And the Priesthood — the Spirit that is within him — will continue to increase until it becomes like a fountain of living water; until it is like the tree of life; until it is one continued source of intelligence and instruction to the individual. (*JD* 3:192.)

The priesthood, properly exercised, encompasses both authority and power. As the fifth article of faith states, it provides authority to "preach the Gospel and administer in the ordinances thereof." It also has the privilege, through harmony and attunement, to draw upon the powers of heaven. This is the power of the priesthood. It is available for performing whatsoever God wills to be done.

Sometimes, however, our vision of the possibilities and potential of the priesthood needs to be enlarged. Such an expansion has been presented to the Melchizedek Priesthood members in these words:

> The scriptures teach us that "Melchizedek was a man of faith who wrought righteousness" and who "obtained peace in Salem" (Joseph Smith Translation, Genesis 14:26, 33). The same passages also teach us that all who are ordained to the same order and calling of priesthood as held by Melchizedek "should have power, by faith, to break mountains, to divide the seas, to dry up waters, to turn them out of their course;
>
> "To put at defiance the armies of nations, to divide the earth, to break every band, to stand in the presence of God; to do all things according to his will, according to his command, subdue principalities and powers; and this by the will of the Son of God which was from before the foundation of the world." (Joseph Smith Translation, Genesis 14:30-31; italics added.) (*Choose You This Day*, p. 93.)

Note in this particular quotation the emphasis that they "should have power, by faith." Where faith is absent, power cannot be present. "Without faith it is impossible to please him [God]." (Hebrews 11:6.) The degree of faith determines the power that may be made available. The power is in the hands of God. He gives it to whomever he will, whenever he will. It is received, however, upon the basis of worthiness. This power is incompatible with domination, criticism, or any degree of unrighteousness.

We must not limit God and forbid him to allow worthy children to receive blessings through their faith and his power, since such blessings are predicated upon faith. We cannot rightly suppose that the power of God can come only through priesthood channels on this side of the veil.

But we can say that it does come through the established priesthood when such priesthood is exercised in righteousness. It is a responsibility for the bearers of this sacred stewardship to develop such attunement that they can know the mind and will of God in any situation. To know that something is the will of God will certainly increase one's assurance that it will be done.

A man of God should be available at all times to be used as a channel for God's power to bless, to heal, and to calm troubled minds and hearts. The authority is a sacred stewardship to act, as called, in the Church. The power is a divine communication that has to be understood, developed, and exercised. It is contingent upon worthiness and upon faith.

The power of God may come and then be absent, depending upon the sensitivity of a man's spirit at any given time or his degree of attunement and faith. Sometimes such conditions require fasting and fervent prayers. At other times such power may fill one's soul almost to the consuming of his flesh.

To be a channel for the power of God, one must have harmonious feelings and faith. This is a requirement. Hence the importance of our continuous nurturing of peace, harmony, and divine receptivity in our lives.

One must have such a degree of harmony that he can ask and receive and know that he knows the will of God for a given situation. And then he must act upon it.

Our responsibility to exercise faith in healing ordinances has been clearly stated by President George Q. Cannon:

> Many of us have not faith enough even to send for the Elders of the Church when any one of our family is sick; but the first thought is, "go for a doctor," as though the gift of healing had been lost in the Church. How many of you feel as if the gift of healing no longer existed in the Church of Christ but that doctors must be sent for and drugs administered? And this among the Latter-day Saints, a people who profess what we do and to whom such glorious promises have been made!

I am scarcely ever called in to administer to a sick person without being told what the doctor is doing and what he says. To me, it is an evidence of a want of faith in the ordinances of God's house and in His promises. To think of a people with the promise made to them that their sick shall be healed, if they will only exercise faith, neglecting this and treating it as though there was no certainty to be attached to it!

It is the same in other directions. We fail to set a proper example before our young people. If I were to send for a doctor, what would be the effect upon my children? Why, they would say, "That is the course my father took, and he is an Elder in the Church and a man of experience; he sent for the doctors, and why should not I? My mother was a good woman, but when one of the children was sick, she sent for a doctor; she did not trust to the ordinance alone; and shall we not send for a doctor? Must it all be faith and no works?" How often do we hear this sort of reasoning?

There is too great a disposition, when sickness enters a household, to send for a doctor. Occasional appeals will be made to the Elders to come and administer, but the two methods are too frequently united — the doctor on the one hand and the Elders on the other.

The experience of those who put their trust in the Lord, and who with careful nursing unite the administering of the ordinance, goes to prove that the Lord has not forgotten His promises. Instances are very common among the faithful Saints of the gift of healing being manifested in a very wonderful manner.

In the breasts of our children, especially, the greatest care should be taken to inculcate faith in this healing ordinance. Where children are thus taught, it is remarkable how strong their faith becomes. . . .

God has not forgotten His promises, and He has not withdrawn Himself from His people. But the Latter-day Saints should make use of these means more frequently than they do, and put more trust in God and less in man's skill. (*Gospel Truth,* 2:185-87.)

Confirming President Cannon's counsel, I recently met a devoted mother of four young children. Her five-year-old boy had a high fever, a sore throat, and swollen tonsils. His father gave him a blessing and a promise of healing.

The next morning this lad complained that his throat was still very sore. His mother calmly said, "Son, your throat shouldn't be sore today. You were promised last night that Heavenly Father would heal it. You'd better go back into your room and claim your blessing."

A few minutes later the boy came out, grinning. His throat was not sore. His fever was down. The swelling was gone. Later that day he went fishing with his father.

Imagine the influence of this experience in his life! He may well grow up to be a man of mighty faith because he had a father who honored his priesthood and a mother who trusted in the promises of the Lord.

*We must seek the ability . . . to
sanctify our motives, desires, feelings and affections, that they may be
pure and holy . . . such a man in his
sphere is perfect, and commands the
blessing of God in all that he does
and wherever he goes.*
(Lorenzo Snow, JD 20:189.)

6

Yes, You Can
Be Perfect—Today

Whenever we speak to anyone about being perfect, the response is usually an incredulous look followed by a torrent of
explanations as to why this is impossible. "After all," he explains,
"only one person who ever lived upon this earth was perfect,
and that was Jesus Christ."

Such a person might do well to read the scriptures with
understanding. He will discover that there are mentioned more
than a dozen specifically-named perfect men in addition to many
"just men made perfect" and the entire City of Enoch and those
who were taken to heaven with Melchizedek.

Recently one of our temple workers related an account of one
of our Brethren who was speaking on perfection before a large
audience. In order to amplify his point, he invited anyone in the
audience who felt that he or she was perfect to stand up and be

recognized. He was pleasantly surprised to see a middle-aged man near the rear of the hall stand up.

"Do you mean to tell me that you think you are perfect?" quieried the speaker.

"No," came the answer. "I am standing up for my wife's first husband!"

It would appear that there are at least some people who feel that being perfect is a distinct possibility!

On another occasion President Heber J. Grant was touring the missions of Europe in 1937. While a group of missionaries was enjoying the evening meal with him in the Berlin mission home, he shared with them one of his most delightful experiences. He let them in on a family secret which he apparently felt might help them in the future when they might choose to make marriage a part of their lives.

It seems that before he and his sweetheart were married, she suggested that they agree to be perfectly frank and honest with each other. Both of them probably had faults and habits that might prove to be irritating or displeasing to the other. But since they both believed in constant improvement, they should agree before their marriage that, rather than enduring each other's vexations, each would bring such irritations to the other's attention as they were encountered. To this arrangement President Grant agreed.

During the first few weeks of their marriage, she brought a number of such items to his attention. He always expressed thanks and vowed that he would try to correct them. As they approached the end of the second month, she reminded him of their bargain and said, "While I have kept up my agreement with you, you have never once mentioned anything displeasing about me."

President Grant replied, "But my dear, you are perfect!" And then, with a twinkle in his eyes, he said, "You know, that's the last time that she ever criticized me."

Accepting Divine Challenges

In a more serious vein, let us examine why most of us usually speak of becoming perfect rather than being perfect. In the scriptures the admonition to be perfect appears at least nine times. Surely the Lord Jesus Christ was not deceiving us when he said, "Be ye therefore perfect, even as your Father which is in heaven is perfect." (Matthew 5:48.) After his resurrection, while speaking to those on the American continent, he included himself in these words: "Therefore I would that ye should be perfect even as I, or your Father who is in heaven is perfect." (3 Nephi 12:48.)

In a masterful discourse at April conference in 1879, Lorenzo Snow outlined the real meaning and challenge of perfection. He presented the obligation of Latter-day Saints to be perfect:

> We learn that the Lord appeared to Abraham and made him very great promises, and that before he was prepared to receive them, a certain requirement was made of him, that he should become perfect before the Lord. And the same requirement was made by the Savior of his disciples . . .
>
> The Latter-day Saints . . . like Abraham . . . are also required to arrive at a state of perfection before the Lord . . . and the Lord . . . has not made a requirement that cannot be complied with. (*JD* 20:187-92.)

Apparently many good people feel that it is a serious sin to think of themselves as perfect. Perhaps that is why they always rationalize by suggesting that the Savior really meant that we should be striving toward becoming perfect rather than being perfect. (In our own household we have always counseled our children that whenever anyone begins to rationalize, they should remember that when you dissect this word, it ends up *rational lies!*)

In addressing the priesthood at the 1972 October conference, President Harold B. Lee used the following expression in regard to considering the Lord's promises:

> Now, there is one thing that I think we should all be mindful of. I was with a group of missionaries in the temple one day. A question was asked by one of the sisters about the Word of Wisdom, concerning the promise made that if one would keep the Word of Wisdom he should run and not be weary and should walk and not faint. And she said, "How could that promise be realized if a person were crippled? How could he receive the blessing that he could run and not be weary, and walk and not faint, if he were crippled?"
>
> I answered her, "Did you ever doubt the Lord? The Lord said that." The trouble with us today, there are too many of us who put

question marks instead of periods after what the Lord says. I want you to think about that.

We shouldn't be concerned about why he said something, or whether or not it can be made so. Just trust the Lord. We don't try to find the answers or explanations. We shouldn't try to spend time explaining what the Lord didn't see fit to explain. We spend useless time.

If you would teach our people to put periods and not question marks after what the Lord has declared, we would say, "It is enough for me to know that is what the Lord said." ("Admonitions for the Priesthood of God," *Ensign*, Jan. 1973, p. 108.)

The difficulty in this matter of perfection lies not with what the Lord said so much as in the definition of *perfection* that some suggest that we should accept. Often such definitions imply continual self-dissatisfaction by striving to fulfill an unattainable concept. Surely this is not what the Lord intended. He never gives any commandments to the children of men that they, with his help, are incapable of fulfilling. So we should establish a more reasonable and attainable definition of *being perfect* if we are to have the necessary motivation for trying to succeed.

Brigham Young offered a simple definition that brings the matter of perfection to a level where we can understand it.

We all occupy diversified stations in the world, and in the kingdom of God. Those who do right, and seek the glory of the Father in heaven, whether their knowledge be little or much, or whether they can do little or much, if they do the very best they know how, they are perfect . . .

. . . "Be ye as perfect as ye can," for that is all we can do tho' it is written, "Be ye perfect as your Father who is in heaven is perfect." To be as perfect as we possibly can according to our knowledge is to be just as perfect as our Father in heaven is. He cannot be any more perfect than he knows how, any more than we. When we are doing as well as we know how in the sphere, and station which we occupy here, we are justified . . . we are as justified as the angels who are before the throne of God. The sin that will cleave to all the posterity of Adam and Eve is, that they have not done as well as they know how! (*Deseret News Weekly*, 31 Aug. 1854, p. 37.)

Such a goal is achievable on a daily basis. Fortunately, the Lord's declaration concerning our perfection uses the term *even as.* This modifies the concept and the divine commandment to practical and reasonable goals.

Perhaps this is one reason why Brigham Young is usually extolled for being so practical, so down-to-earth. By the same token, he also provides a challenge by letting us know what the real sin will be when we approach the judgment seat of God.

President Joseph F. Smith lends support to those concepts and adds the term "righteous" to focus upon the most important single ingredient.

> . . . it is given to us to be as perfect in the sphere in which we are called . . . to act, as it is for the Father in heaven to be pure and righteous in the more exalted sphere in which he acts. We will find in the scriptures the words of the Savior himself to his disciples, in which he required that they should be perfect, even as their Father in heaven is perfect; that they should be righteous, even as he is righteous. (Joseph F. Smith, *Gospel Doctrine*, 5th ed. [Salt Lake City: Deseret Book Co., 1939], p. 132.)

This certainly presents a noble challenge and one that we should accept gladly, realizing, as we do, that God never requires anything of us without the willingness to provide the vision and the power to accomplish it. Remember this: You are a divine creation. You are created, in both body and spirit, in God's image and likeness.

Doing Your Best Each Day

For purposes of this book, we are not considering perfection in the absolute sense but in a person's commitment to do his very best each day of his life.

In this light even Jesus Christ who as Jehovah was perfect qualifies, since John testified that "he received not of the fulness at the first, but received grace for grace; And he received not of the fulness at first, but continued from grace to grace, until he received a fulness." (D&C 93:12-13.) And the Apostle Paul records that "Though he were a Son, yet learned he obedience by the things which he suffered." (Hebrews 5:8.) So the perfection of Jesus was still relative to the perfection of his (and our) Father in heaven, even as he and the Father must consider our perfection to be.

Perfection is a road, not a destination. It is doing your best wherever you are and whatever you do. It is doing the best you know how to do, according to your knowledge at that time. But a week from now, or a year from now, you will have gained more knowledge and experience, and then more will be expected.

A young mother recently was very much relieved as she came to understand this principle. "I have had a perfect day. I have done this and this." She enumerated the things she had accomplished. "Of course, I didn't get other things done, but I did the best I could."

Instead of condemning herself for the things she had not done, which would have denied her the Spirit of the Lord, she was happy and had a productive day which she pronounced to be perfect.

Perfection, then, becomes a way of life; it is not a measure of achievement but an attitude toward achievement. A person's degree of perfection is always relative to his degree of knowledge and ability at any given time. Thus each individual will be judged on his own merits in relation to his ability to do.

Noblesse oblige: Because you are of noble birth, you are expected (obliged) to act a certain way. This applies to us. Because we are who we are, certain things are expected of us. And because we are who we are, we can achieve them. Therefore, let us do them.

With these guidelines to sustain us, let us now examine some ideas that beckon us to move "forward and upward" as President Spencer W. Kimball has challenged us to do.

Opening New Vistas

Let us remember that love is the most perfecting quality in the universe. Through it is fulfilled "all the law and the prophets."

Another important quality is patience. James makes this promise concerning patience:

> My brethren, count it all joy when ye fall into divers temptations;
> Knowing this, that the trying of your faith worketh patience.
> But let patience have her perfect work, that ye may be perfect and entire, wanting nothing. (James 1:2-4.)

A third essential ingredient is persistence.
The following insights portray our moving toward perfection:

The Path of Perfection

1) To be (become like our Heavenly Father)
   Or not to be (become like Him),
   That is the question (each one of us must decide).

   If we do not think about it, it will not happen.
   If we do think about it, it may happen.

2) It starts as a longing in your heart.
   Then as your mind comes to recognize this desire,
   It searches for ways and means for it to be accomplished.

   Such mental activity then stimulates your feelings with hope.
   As an inner excitement grows . . . your anticipation expands.

   Thus does yearning become excitement,
   And excitement becomes anticipation,
   And your anticipation becomes faith
   As you begin to do things to bring about your desire.

3) Then your desire stimulates thoughts
   And the two together stimulate action.
   Action, in turn, will increase your faith,
       your desire, and your thoughts.

   Thus each can stimulate the others
       for greater and greater attainment.

4) Your mind acts as a researcher, searching out ways and means.
   It serves as an organizer . . . and a discipliner . . .
   Pointing the way for the action.

   Your feelings are what impel you toward actions.
   As you see the results of your efforts,
   They will either offer greater encouragement,
   Or they can result in discouragement,
       if you are not on your guard.

   Discouragement is a "booby trap" . . .
   Sucking many a man down — like quicksand —
       away from his golden dream.

5) We must learn from our experience . . .
   Not be stopped by it!

Success is the result of having learned from our errors . . .
Correcting our errors . . .
And trying again . . . and again . . . and again.
One cannot fail until he stops trying!

6) As we come to a "roadblock" —
If our desire holds strong —
Our minds will seek alternative ways and means.

Remember . . . a setback may stop our action . . . for a
moment,
But it cannot stop our desire and our thoughts
Which produced the action in the first place . . .
Unless we permit it to do so.

Experience consists of success and failure.
Be grateful when you fail.
It can teach you how not to accomplish your goal,
And it can become a catalyst for greater desire and effort . . .
Adjusted now by your experience to date.

7) We can also learn from the experience of others,
But we cannot learn for others.
Each of us must learn for ourselves the lessons of life.
But our way can be made easier
If we profit from the experience
of those who have gone before.

8) To be(come like our Heavenly Father)
Or not to be(come like Him).
That is the question (every man must answer for himself)!

(June Andrew Babbel, unpublished manuscript.)

Key to Eternal Life

Early in his ministry the Prophet Joseph Smith made a declaration that will gladden the hearts of all who are now willing to
be perfect in accordance with the pattern outlined. What he said
will fortify your determination as it did for those who heard it
when he uttered these memorable words:

We consider that God has created man with a mind capable of
instruction, and a faculty which may be enlarged in proportion to
the heed and diligence given to the light communicated from
heaven to the intellect: and that the nearer man approaches perfection, the clearer are his views, and the greater his enjoyments,

till he has overcome the evils of his life and lost every desire for sin; and like the ancients, arrives at that point of faith where he is wrapped in the power and glory of his Maker, and is caught up to dwell with Him. (*DHC* 2:8.)

Finally, let us consider and accept this forceful challenge given us by the Prophet Joseph Smith:

I would exhort you to go on and continue to call upon God until you make your calling and election sure for yourselves, by obtaining this more sure word of prophecy. . . .

Oh, I beseech you to go forward, go forward and make your calling and election sure! (*DHC* 5:389; 6:365.)

*I promise you, as a servant of the
living God, that every man and woman
who obeys the commandments of God
shall prosper; that every promise
made of God shall be fulfilled upon
their heads, and that they will grow
and increase in wisdom, light, knowledge, intelligence, and, above all,
in the testimony of the Lord Jesus
Christ.*
(Heber J. Grant, *Improvement Era*,
1940, 42:585.)

7

Claiming Divine Promises

The promises of the Lord to all mankind are recorded in the holy scriptures. In addition, a person may learn of specific individual promises from four primary sources: a patriarchal blessing, a special father's or priesthood blessing, an administration for illness, or a special blessing when being set apart for specific Church responsibilities.

Have you received a patriarchal blessing from your own father or from an ordained patriarch? You are entitled to both.

When did you last review this blessing to determine your progress in realizing the promises contained?

What kind of challenges were given? How have you met them?

What special gifts were you promised? What expectations were you counseled to achieve? What have you done to bring these forth in your life?

How have you applied yourself so that your belief in these promises might become unshakable conviction through knowledge that you are receiving them?

Do you feel that the special gifts mentioned in your patriarchal blessing, such as the gift of faith, or the gift of healing, will be received by waiting for the Lord to give them to you? For many years this was my expectation. Then I learned that these gifts were waiting for me to develop them.

For each one of us our patriarchal blessing is a personalized unveiling of expectations and promises taken from our own eternal book of life. This should become our immediate focus for claiming divine promises.

Realizing Personal Divine Promises

One day my wife's father invited us to see the inside of one of the large sugar elevators at the local sugar factory where he was the chief chemist.

When we entered the inside of this large storage elevator, which appeared to be at least three hundred feet high, we observed that the only means of getting to the top was by using a continuously running belt that extended from the base to the top. On the belt were small platforms for your feet and bars to hold with your hands. My wife declined to try it. I went with the plant foreman to explore what was at the top of this huge shaft.

The foreman and I were examining the powerful machinery that continuously moves the sugar to keep it fresh and uncaked until shipment. It was hard to hear him explain what was taking place unless he spoke loudly.

All at once we heard a scream for help. I looked over to see my wife going over the top of the belt, heading toward a three-hundred-foot drop down the shaft. She did not know how to stop the mechanism. In desperation she grabbed the side of the belt to hang on and threw her body out from the belt as she screamed.

We rushed over. The foreman quickly yanked the emergency cord to stop the belt. One of my wife's feet had just reached the edge of the large circular hole, and her hands were six inches from being crushed or severed by the wheels through which the belt passed.

We grabbed her and pulled her to safety. Her first remark as she found herself in my arms was, "I'm thankful for my patriarchal blessing!" This blessing contains the promise that she will never suffer serious harm or accident as long as she adheres to the Word of Wisdom. By obeying the Word of Wisdom she was automatically fulfilling the requirement for the blessing before it was needed.

This is an example of a conditional promise. Many of the promises of the Lord are conditional, and we cannot receive them without fulfilling the condition.

Other promises, such as those in blessings of the sick or in settings apart for special callings, may be received, but we must claim them. Perhaps a case in my own life will illustrate what is meant by claiming your blessing.

I had returned from my special mission in Europe after World War II. There I had assisted Elder Ezra Taft Benson and Elder Alma Sonne with the mammoth task of distributing welfare supplies and securing needed rehabilitation for our Saints in Europe, the Near East, and South Africa. A physician friend of mine declared that I could not have gone through that experience without having suffered severe physical problems, which would account for my having lost over 40 pounds of weight from my normal 165 pounds. He asked me to come to his office for a free physical examination.

His fears were confirmed. He discovered that both of my lungs had contracted tuberculosis. Since neither lung could be collapsed while the other regained its strength, my condition was serious.

When he reported his findings, I was not dismayed. I reminded the doctor that Elder Alma Sonne had given me a blessing just prior to returning home. In this blessing I was promised that I would not suffer any serious illness or physical problem as a result of my work in Europe. Then I said:

"Doc, I have a contract to complete with the General Foods Corporation in Rochester, New York. While I am there I am going to claim this blessing. If you feel I have need for medical treatment when I return, I'll consider it. But meanwhile I expect to claim my blessing." He reluctantly agreed.

I had been in Rochester about two weeks. The snow was deep and the weather blustery and cold. A friend loaned me his car so I could drive to Palmyra early on a Sunday to visit the Sacred Grove near the Joseph Smith home. I had to break trail to the grove, since no one was venturing to visit there in such weather.

After looking around I found a large tree that provided some shelter for me from the swirling snow and harsh wind. Here I knelt and poured out my soul to the Lord. I reminded Him of the blessing which I had been given and informed Him that I had come to this spot to claim that blessing which I desperately desired and needed. How long I spent there I do not recall, but as I left, my soul was at peace. I experienced divine assurance as only God can give.

Before I ended my six-week contract, I had X-rays of my lungs taken at the Rochester General hospital. When I returned home I took these to my physician. After he examined them he said, "I'm afraid they gave you the wrong films." I assured him that they were correct and were so certified. However, he insisted on examining me under the fluoroscope and then took additional X-rays. As these were scrutinized, he said incredulously, "Well, I guess you have claimed your blessing. Your lungs appear to be as healthy as when you were born. There is no evidence to indicate that you ever had tuberculosis, so I won't record it in your medical history."

May I urge that when you receive such a promise in a blessing that you not only live for it, but also expect it and then claim it. Some people are not aware that this is necessary. My own experience has assured me that the Lord is ready and willing to honor such claims when they are presented.

When we discussed building powerful faith, we considered that faith comes into being only at the point of action. We also suggested that if it makes a man work and keep on working, it is genuine. Let me recount an example of how this principle applies in a real-life situation.

During the last two years of my military career I was in charge of the largest ROTC (Reserve Officers' Training Corps) unit in the San Francisco area. My unit consisted of two 60-piece bands and a cadre of 320 cadets. I had to handle this unit alone because of the shortage of available manpower.

In 1945 my unit was assigned to handle all the official cere-monial functions for those who met in San Francisco to draft the United Nations charter. During this rather hectic time I was also endeavoring to develop some rifle teams to compete in the Pacific Coast rifle team matches sponsored by the National Rifle Association.

Although I had achieved a degree of skill with some weapons, I was never what you might term an expert. One afternoon after rifle team practice, the captain of my first team (I had three teams of five riflemen each) and the colonel in charge of the battalion challenged each other to a match. Since they were keen rivals, I agreed to such a match. I was to be the judge.

Their performance was miserable. I declared it to be "no contest." Then they both began to complain about the rifle they had used. So I asked them to load the rifle with five shells and let me zero it in. They were viewing the target through sighting scopes as I fired.

By some kind of luck, my first shot hit the dead center of the bullseye. The next four shots went through the same hole, en-larging it slightly. They couldn't believe it. Neither could I!

Before the next day ended, word had spread through the unit that I was as expert as the fabled Annie Oakley. From that moment on all fifteen riflemen decided to follow my instructions implicitly. I worked hard with them. And I set standards far beyond what riflemen might ordinarily be expected to achieve. But they didn't know that! The result? The three teams placed first, second, and third in the Pacific Coast rifle matches. They didn't know it couldn't be done! They had complete confidence in me and in my ability to train them properly. The results were astounding!

I mention this account because when we are dealing with the promises of God, we may be sure that he will fulfill them if we do our part. And we must approach the fulfillment of these promises with the eagerness and trust that these young riflemen exhibited.

Why do we not receive the blessings we have been promised?

It could be because we are afraid we are not worthy of them. This is fear. Or it may be that we do not really believe that they were intended for us or that the Lord would grant them under the circumstances. This is unbelieving.

John the Revelator had a few words to say about such attitudes.

> He that overcometh shall inherit all things; and I will be his God, and he shall be my son.
>
> But the fearful, and unbelieving, and the abominable, and murderers, and whoremongers, and sorcerers, and idolaters, and all liars, shall have their part in the lake which burneth with fire and brimstone: which is the second death! (Revelation 21:7-8; see also D&C 63:17.)

Do you realize where the fearful and unbelieving will be? With the whoremongers, and sorcerers, and liars. "For God hath not given us the spirit of fear." (2 Timothy 1:7; see also D&C 67:3.)

The important thing is to keep on loving the Lord and, trusting in His love for us, continuously move forward. Certainly the blessings of those who overcome or fulfill the divine promises exceed our present expectations. By contrast the fearful and unbelieving will suffer the second death. Our choice, therefore, should be an easy one. Let us choose to overcome fear and unbelief.

Keys to Claiming Blessings or Promises

Some promises of God are conditional. We must fulfill the condition.

Some promises of God must be claimed. We must claim them.

Other promises of God require implicit active faith and persistence. We must keep trying.

> Behold, I say unto you that whoso believeth in Christ, doubting nothing, whatsoever he shall ask the Father in the name of Christ it shall be granted him; and this promise is unto all even unto the ends of the earth. (Mormon 9:21.)

It should be a reasonable assumption that if we come to God, doubting nothing, we will automatically do whatever is required.

And then we will fulfill the conditions. This is what we should apply to every promise. Not only will this enable us to gain the added knowledge, but also it will fortify our assurance and we will literally realize that which we have been promised.

To hear about God, promises, and conditions may become a part of a person's beliefs, but until he experiences these for himself, they can never become a part of his actual knowledge. Such knowledge requires personal experience.

We do not realize the promises of the Lord by merely hearing about them. We receive them by seeking them in humble prayer and petition. We must also have a burning desire to realize them and a willingness to fulfill whatever requirements are specified. We must claim the promises to make them ours.

In choosing this course we must not only be steadfast, but also we must be acting for the right reasons and with the right spirit or attitude. The Apostle Paul set this requirement sharply before us in his famous treatise on charity, which the Book of Mormon identifies as "the pure love of Christ." (Moroni 7:47.) In order to understand clearly the kind of feelings we should have in accepting this challenge, note carefully this warning:

> And though I bestow all my goods to feed the poor, and though I give my body to be burned, and have not charity [the pure love of Christ], it profiteth me nothing. (1 Corinthians 13:3.)

If we undertake this quest of overcoming with fear or anxiety or with hope of great gain, it profiteth us nothing. On the other hand, if we do so out of love for God with all our heart, might, mind, and strength, we demonstrate the sincerity of our feelings and attitude. With such love the quest will be a glorious experience and the promises are sure.

What, then, are the keys for claiming blessings or promises?

1. Having a firm faith — doubting nothing.

2. Doing all things with the right attitude — the pure love of Christ.

3. Steadfastness of purpose — persistence.

Discovering Divine Promises

In the scriptures the promises of God are usually based upon certain conditions. We must not only have faith in the promises, but also we must fulfill the conditions pertaining to them. Consider Peter's fitting introduction as we begin our search for the promises: "Give diligence to make your calling and election sure: for if ye do these things, ye shall never fall." (2 Peter 1:10.)

What a challenge! And what a glorious promise!

Obviously such a course takes constant productive effort. However, if we realize that "all things are possible to him that believeth," (Mark 9:23) it can be an exciting journey.

Since we are eternal beings and actual sons and daughters of God—his greatest handiwork—is any other course worthy of our efforts toward fulfilling our measure of creation? This has been repeated throughout this book, but until we accept this truth and begin to act "as if," we will remain unfulfilled or barren.

Where shall we begin our search for the promises? In addition to those found in our personal blessings, promises will be found throughout the sacred scriptures and writings of apostles and prophets, both ancient and modern. As you search the scriptures, write down the promises. You may wish to follow the pattern that will be shown later in this chapter, where a number of promises are listed along with their requirements for fulfillment. You will find that your search for the promises will provide a rich incentive. However, until you fulfill the conditions they require, you cannot realize the joy that comes through achieving the glorious divine promises of God.

A dynamic, living faith must accompany every step of your program to learn and put into practice these promises.

After you have written down the promises, examine their conditions. Remember always the Lord's promise that "I, the Lord, am bound when ye do what I say; but when ye do not what I say, ye have no promise." (D&C 82:10.) If your faith in the Lord Jesus Christ is genuine, you know he will keep his promise. Are you, in turn, happy and anxious to meet his requirements in a spirit of gratitude and love? The spirit with which you seek such fulfillment will determine whether this will be a blessing, an unfruitful exercise, or a burden.

Abraham sought diligently after the promises of the fathers, and his lifelong task was to fulfill the conditions and claim the promises. He lived less than four thousand years ago. Yet modern scripture says this about him, as well as his son Isaac, and his grandson Jacob, or Israel:

> Abraham . . . as Isaac also and Jacob did none other things than that which they were commanded; and because they did none other things than that which they were commanded, they have entered into their exaltation, according to the promises, and sit upon thrones, and are not angels, but are gods." (D&C 132:37.)

Here is evidence that man can become exalted and achieve godhood, not in eons and eons of time, but in less than four thousand years! Measured in terms of eternity, that is hardly a drop in the bucket.

The journey to exaltation is the most exciting and wonderful experience you can undertake. With each positive step the way becomes more meaningful and rewarding.

Let us proceed with the job of finding the promises, internalizing them, and then fulfilling them in our daily lives.

Joseph Smith found a promise, believed it, and as a result had an experience that changed the world.

> If any of you lack wisdom, let him ask of God, that giveth to all men liberally, and upbraideth not; and it shall be given him. (James 1:5.)

Some people feel that this promise was recorded specifically for the use of the Prophet Joseph Smith. Not so. This promise is for all men. God wants us to ask him when we lack wisdom and not those who can impart only human wisdom to us. Joseph Smith's action provides a powerful example of how to claim a promise of God.

Incorporating Divine Promises Within Ourselves

As we begin our task of having the fulfillment of divine promises become a part of our lives, it is profitable to reinforce our understanding of what will really be required. In addition to faith and persistence, remember that one additional quality is necessary for all of our efforts to be effective and acceptable before the Lord. This is the quality, above all others, that our mortal experience was meant to develop to a divine level. I am speaking of love or charity, which is the pure love of Christ. Never lose sight of the fact that love, which is the subject of the first and second great commandments, is that quality upon which all the law and the prophets hang and through which all the law and the prophets are fulfilled.

God expects us to do all that we can do through love. He does not and will not require more than this from anyone. Divine love is the great lesson we must learn in this life. As it is applied, the very powers of heaven will come to our assistance so we may honorably fulfill whatever we are undertaking to accomplish. With such assistance we cannot fail.

An examination of the many divine promises that have been given may lead you to feel that you cannot possibly fulfill them all. It is not necessary to be concerned with all the promises at the same time. Instead, choose one promise that appeals to you. Live for it. Acting upon any of the promises of the Lord will increase the Spirit in your life and serve as a purifying influence. It will also keep you on the Lord's side of the line. As this continues, you will discover that you have not fulfilled just one promise, but you may have automatically met the requirements for many of them.

Remember that perfection is a growing process, a gradual increase in your ability to choose the will of the Lord rather than your own.

Let us examine a number of divine promises so we can learn to identify the requirements and make them a part of our daily living. The following pattern may be useful in helping you separate the conditions from the promises.

Reference	Conditions	Promises
Mark 9:23	If thou canst believe . . .	all things are possible to him that believeth.
Mark 11:24; see also John 15:7	What things soever ye desire, when ye pray, believe that ye receive them,	and ye shall have them.

You will observe that desire and belief on your part are prime requisites. The Lord has promised that he will grant whatever you desire, but you must so completely accept that promise that there shall be no doubts. You must act as if you knew your success was already assured — and it shall be! Those who have done so can testify that this is how it works.

Reference	Conditions	Promises
John 14:12-15	. . . He that believeth on me, the works that I do shall he do also; and greater works than these shall he do.	
	And whatsoever ye shall ask in my name,	that will I do . . .
	If ye shall ask any thing in my name,	I will do it.

This promise is an exciting one. In a Gospel Essentials class in Sunday School we had three lovely middle-aged ladies present for the first time. The instructor was teaching from Elder James E. Talmage's *Articles of Faith* and was intent upon drawing a clear distinction between faith and belief. One of these ladies commented, "But the Bible distinctly promises 'Believe on the Lord Jesus Christ, and thou shalt be saved' (Acts 16:31.), so I do not agree that we must have faith to be saved."

A rather heated exchange of arguments resulted. I could sense that these guests were at the point of leaving the class, so I stood up and said to the instructor, "I agree with these ladies that all you need is belief." Whereupon the instructor responded, "Brother Babbel, you can't mean that!"

I assured him that I meant just that. Then I turned to these ladies and asked, "Are you willing to accept the Savior's own definition of belief?" To this they readily assented. Then I quoted John 14:12 and continued, "You will note how the Savior emphasized that the belief he required of us would enable us to do the works that he had done and even greater works. A belief that leads to that kind of performance will get you to the highest level of exaltation in the kingdom of God. It is even more demanding than the faith which our instructor has been trying to explain."

Many people are disturbed by the statement, "and greater works than these shall ye do . . ." How is this possible? What did Jesus mean?

We accept the statement in Moses 1:39 that the work and glory of God is to bring to pass the immortality and eternal life of man. Jesus, through his atonement, has insured the resurrection either of exaltation or salvation (the first resurrection) or that of damnation (the later and final resurrections). This is a primary work of God.

However, the greater works—those resulting in eternal life (which is the glory of God and is proclaimed to be the greatest of all of the gifts of God to man)—can be achieved only by mortals themselves as they willingly conform themselves to the divine image by applying the teachings and the power available to them through Jesus Christ, that is, by the righteous application of their God-given gift of agency.

In addition, until Jesus Christ opened the prison doors of the spirit world during his visit there between the time of his crucifixion and his resurrection, the work for the myriads of deceased souls who had no opportunity to accept the gospel during their mortality could not be done. That work was subsequently inaugurated, and it is now performed in modern temples of the Lord. Only we, the living, can perform this necessary work in behalf of those who have passed on; and by doing so we can become "saviors on mount Zion."

Thus do we have the opportunity to perform "greater works" which Jesus referred to but which he could not do, since his mortal life had to be and was terminated in order that those works could be accomplished. So this challenge and promise carry more meaning than most mortals have dared to believe.

In short, some of these greater works pertain to our gaining eternal life through righteousness and becoming saviors on mount Zion through our genealogical and temple work in behalf of those deceased.

Reference	Conditions	Promises
Proverbs 3:5-6	Trust in the Lord with all thine heart; and lean not unto thine own understanding. In all thy ways acknowledge him,	and he shall direct thy paths.

This is one of my favorites. It really works. I love it. Try it.

We need to identify the things which are of God and those which are from the adversary. Despise those that come from the wrong source and you shall rule over them on every occasion and stay on the Lord's side of the line.

Reference	Conditions	Promises
Isaiah 26:3	whose mind is stayed on thee: because he trusteth in thee.	Thou wilt keep him in perfect peace,
Psalm 55:22	Cast thy burden upon the Lord,	and he shall sustain thee: He shall never suffer the righteous to be moved.

Here the Lord is inviting us to cast our burdens upon him. He is an expert in handling them and is willing to do so. However, when we do, we must avoid the temptation to look over his shoulder, so to speak, to make certain that he is handling them. The minute we do this, we show lack of faith and the burdens will be returned to us multiplied and left for us to handle them. Don't ever make this mistake. When you have given your burdens to the Lord, as he has asked, trust him and they will be handled.

Reference	Conditions	Promises
D&C 6:7	Seek not for riches but for wisdom,	and behold, the mysteries of God shall be unfolded unto you, and then shall

you be made rich. Behold,
he that hath eternal life is
rich.

This is a wonderful promise and a gentle reminder to keep
our priorities in life in proper perspective.

Reference	Conditions	Promises
D&C 64:23	. . . he that is tithed	shall not be burned at his coming.

This is the best "fire insurance policy" on the face of the
earth.

Reference	Conditions	Promises
John 14:23	If a man love me, he will keep my words:	and my Father will love him, and we will come unto him, and make our abode with him.

Do you realize what he is promising? This pertains to this
life. Joseph Smith explains this scripture as follows: "The
appearing of the Father and the Son, in that verse, is a personal
appearance; and the idea that the Father and the Son dwell in a
man's heart is an old sectarian notion, and is false." (D&C 130:3.)

Reference	Conditions	Promises
D&C 88:67; *see also* Revelation 3:21-22	If your eye be single to my glory,	your whole bodies shall be filled with light, and there shall be no darkness in you; and that body which is filled with light comprehendeth all things.

Add this to the preceding promise and you may begin to perceive what the Apostle Paul meant when he said, "Let this mind
be in you, which was also in Christ Jesus: Who, being in the
form of God, thought it not robbery to be equal with God."
(Philippians 2:5-6.)

Reference	Conditions	Promises
D&C 14:7	If you keep my commandments and endure to the end	you shall have eternal life, which gift is the greatest of all the gifts of God.
D&C 78:19	And he who receiveth all things with thankfulness	shall be made glorious; and the things of this earth shall be added unto him, even an hundred fold, yea, more.
D&C 88:68	Sanctify yourselves that your minds become single to God,	and the days will come that you shall see him; for he will unveil his face unto you, and it shall be in his own time, and in his own way, and according to his own will.

Experiencing Fulfillment of Divine Promises

How many other promises can you find? The divine promises we have listed here are only a small portion of those you will discover as you search for them. However, only as you begin to incorporate them in your life and live by their conditions will the promises begin to be fulfilled. As each promise is granted, your faith and eager compliance will grow. Your ability to receive will also increase. Once you have overcome your inertia, this entire process will be accelerated and your blessings will be multiplied.

Be patient, persistent, faithful, and enduring. The promises of the Lord are genuine. They have been realized by many others and if you follow the example of our Lord and Master, Jesus Christ, they will also be fulfilled in your life. Stay on the Lord's side of the line. Do your best and you will not fail.

As you search for and live for the promises, you will become eligible to receive the same blessings that have been realized by your progenitors, Abraham, Isaac, and Jacob.

If ye love me,
keep my commandments.
And I will pray the Father,
and he shall give you
    another Comforter,
that he may abide with you
for ever.
(John 14:15-16.)

8

We Will Make
Our Abode With Him

In his masterful discourse on the three degrees of glory, Elder Melvin J. Ballard makes this significant comment:

> Do you comprehend . . . the privilege of dwelling in the presence of God and his Christ forever and ever? . . . to have in the world, during his ministry, for three brief years the Lord Jesus Christ? . . . It was the most wonderful privilege the world has ever had.
>
> What would you give tonight for the privilege of standing in the presence of the Son for five minutes? You would give all your earthly possessions for that privilege.
>
> Then can you comprehend the full meaning and significance of the statement that those who gain celestial glory will have the privilege of dwelling in the presence of the Father and the Son forever and ever? . . . It is beyond price and earthly possessions. Even the giving of life itself would be a trifle for the privilege to dwell forever and ever in the presence of the Father and the Son. (*The Three*

Degrees of Glory [Salt Lake City: Magazine Printing and Publishing, 1975], p. 14.)

"Has anyone actually ever seen God face to face and talked with him?" you may ask. Of course! There are several accounts in the Holy Bible and in the Book of Mormon of individuals from the days of Adam to the coming of Christ in the meridian of time, and since the resurrection of Jesus Christ, who have seen him or heard his voice. And you may, too!

Thousands became acquainted with Jesus Christ during his ministry upon the earth. Thousands witnessed him in person as the resurrected Lord stood here upon the American continent. Additional people had this same privilege in Palestine.

According to his divine promise, he is willing to acquaint such people with his and our Heavenly and Eternal Father. We know that Adam and Eve were visited by both the Father and the Son before their expulsion from the Garden of Eden.

It may come as a surprise to some that we have as a matter of historical record the testimonies of a number of people in this dispensation who have seen the Father as well as others who have beheld Jesus Christ. Following are some who have beheld the Father or heard his voice: The Prophet Joseph Smith, Sidney Rigdon, Newel Knight, Zebedee Coltrin, Lyman Wight, Philo Dibble, and Alfred Douglas Young. Their accounts are thrilling to read.

The list of those who have beheld or conversed with the Savior, Jesus Christ, may be lengthy, but the following left their witness in writing: the Prophet Joseph Smith, Sidney Rigdon, Oliver Cowdery, Newel Knight, Lyman Wight, Zebedee Coltrin, Philo Dibble, John Murdock, Alfred Douglas Young, Martin Harris, Alexander Neibaur, President Lorenzo Snow, Elder Orson F. Whitney, President George Q. Cannon, President Joseph F. Smith, Elder Melvin J. Ballard, President George F. Richards, and President David O. McKay.

Brief excerpts and some full accounts of these visits are found in the latter part of this chapter and are provided to motivate you in your search for such fulfillment. We hope that when your experience takes place, you may also record it so as to inspire others.

In view of some of the promises given by Jesus Christ, several of which suggest that this privilege is available to all who sincerely desire it, why hasn't this become a more widespread personal experience?

First of all, most people feel that this couldn't possibly happen, particularly to them. They are right. It won't, especially to them.

Second, many people believe that God is a mysterious, unknowable, three-in-one being composed of a spirit essence that cannot be beheld or comprehended. These people by their attitude also deny themselves this privilege.

Finally, considerable numbers do not believe in such visitations, and they declare that there is no God. These persons also forfeit this opportunity.

Our purpose here, however, is to discover how this glorious opportunity may be realized by us.

Discerning the Pathway

Our sacred quest to establish a meaningful relationship with Deity must begin through an acceptance of this declaration:

> But without faith it is impossible to please him: for he that cometh to God must believe that he is, and that he is a rewarder of them that diligently seek him. (Hebrews 11:6.)

Without this foundation, our quest might as well end right here. If you are willing to accept this first requirement, then let us continue our search.

To trust God, we must know something about him. The more we know about God, the more we can trust him. But how can we learn more about God?

1. Through studying and pondering the sacred scriptures.

2. Through comprehending the declarations of prophets, apostles, and others who have enjoyed divine revelation.

3. Through learning more about the intricacies of nature and/or ourselves.

4. Through fervent two-way prayer and personal divine revelation.

Scripture study is one of the most important ways a person can come to know about God. (1 Nephi 19:22-23; 2 Timothy 3:15-17.) This is a personal undertaking.

The Old Testament, like other scriptures, teaches the doctrine of Christ who, as Jehovah, is the God of Abraham, Isaac, and Jacob.

Through our modern-day prophets we receive many profound insights. Let us examine parts of three discussions:

> God himself, who sits enthroned in yonder heavens, is a man like unto one of yourselves, that is the great secret. If the vail was rent to-day, and the great God, who holds this world in its orbit, and upholds all things by his power; if you were to see him to-day, you would see him in all the person, image and very form as a man; for Adam was created in the very fashion and image of God; Adam received instruction, walked, talked and conversed with him, as one man talks and communes with another.
>
> . . . the simple and first principles of the gospel, to know for a certainty the character of God, that we may converse with him as one man with another, and that God himself; the Father of us all dwelt on an earth the same as Jesus Christ himself did. (*Times and Seasons* 5:613-14, Aug. 15, 1844.)

> I want to tell you, each and every one of you, that you are well acquainted with God our heavenly Father, or the great Eloheim. You are all well acquainted with Him, for there is not a soul of you but what has lived in His house and dwelt with Him year after year; and yet you are seeking to become acquainted with Him, when the fact is, you have merely forgotten what you did know.
>
> There is not a person here to-day but what is a son or a daughter of that Being. In the spirit world their spirits were first begotten and brought forth, and they lived there with their parents for ages before they came here. This, perhaps, is hard for many to believe, but it is the greatest nonsense in the world not to believe it. If you do not believe it, cease to call Him Father; and when you pray, pray to some other character. (*JD* 4:216.)

> If any of us could now see the God we are striving to serve — if we could see our Father who dwells in the heavens, we should learn that we are as well acquainted with him as we are with our earthly father; and he would be as familiar to us in the expression of his countenance, and we should be ready to embrace him and

fall upon his neck and kiss him, if we had the privilege. And still we, unless the vision of the Spirit is opened to us, know nothing about God. You know much about him, if you did but realize it. And there is no other one item that will so much astound you, when your eyes are opened in eternity, as to think that you were so stupid in the body. (*JD* 8:30.)

The more we learn of the intricacies of nature, our earth, and of our bodies, the more we marvel at the wisdom of that Master Intelligence who designed them for our good. (Psalm 19:1; 8:3-9.)

Our vital communication line with God is prayer. Prayer is an indispensable ingredient in establishing a meaningful relationship with Deity. While Jesus Christ has asked us to pray to our Father in heaven, he has always taught that all of his efforts must be in complete harmony with and have the approval of our Father in heaven.

To fully accomplish its divinely planned objective, prayer must be "co-munication," not "mono-munication." Its most priceless benefits come from free interchange of ideas, thoughts, feelings, and petitions. Unless it becomes an effective medium, like the telephone, where responses are generated on both ends of the connection, it lacks effectiveness in achieving its major purpose.

In connection with this powerful aid, Brigham Young offered some pertinent counsel that we should consider:

> Let all persons be fervent in prayer until they know the things of God for themselves and become certain that they are walking in the path that leads to everlasting life; then will envy, the child of ignorance, vanish, and there will be no disposition in any man to place himself above another; for such a feeling meets no countenance in the order of heaven. (*JD* 9:150.)

> If we draw near to him, he will draw near to us; if we seek him early, we shall find him; if we apply our minds faithfully and diligently, day by day, to know and understand the mind and will of God, it is as easy as, yes, I will say easier than it is to know the minds of each other, for to know and understand our own being is to know and understand God and his being. (*JD* 13:312.)

If you have put into your life the principles, laws, and evidences presented in previous chapters, you should now understand how to increase faith and how to grow in personal revelation as well as how to use your agency in such a manner that you may realize the things you fervently desire.

Applying the Power of Visualization

As he [man] thinketh in his heart, so is he. (Proverbs 23:7.)

We mentioned this scripture earlier in this book. It illustrates an important faculty of mankind. We literally become what we think about all day long. Our thoughts fashion our feelings; our feelings shape our actions.

In the same manner, each of us possesses, to some degree, the faculty of imagination. What a man can believe, perceive, or visualize can and will become a reality if it is coupled with faith and persistence.

We can use this power of visualization in several important ways. First of all, visualize in your mind the Father leaning over your shoulder to listen to your prayers. Pray as though he is there in person, for, in reality, that may be the case more often than you realize.

When you are faced with a problem or a choice, visualize what you feel the Savior would do in such a circumstance. Then visualize yourself doing it. You will soon discover that this process makes him seem to be an ever-present companion, which, in fact, he really is if you invite him in this manner to be such.

I am acquainted with choice people who, when administering to the sick, visualize Jesus in attendance. They see him with his hands placed upon the head of the person giving the blessing. Having been in the position of pronouncing many blessings, I have experienced a feeling like hands upon my own head, pouring in their love and power so that it might flow through me into the person being blessed. This is an humbling and a sobering sensation.

As you visualize in this manner, notice how your feelings are affected and how your spirit is charged with an inflowing power. Do not underestimate this power of visualization. It can help you achieve the kind of readiness and attunement you will need to be receptive when the time arrives for you to meet the Savior in whatever manner he will reveal himself unto you.

One of the sweetest experiences I can recall during the time I spent with Elder Ezra Taft Benson in Europe right after World War II was when we knelt in prayer with Elder Walter Stover who had been assigned to preside over the Berlin, Germany Mission. When Elder Stover acted as mouth for our prayer together, he was speaking directly to his Father, and his prayer brought Elder Benson and myself to tears. We hesitated to open our eyes during prayer because his humility and sincerity literally pulled the presence of God into our midst. What sacred moments we shared in this way!

> You begin knowing about Jesus
> Then as you realize the extent of His love for you,
> You can come to love Him.
> As you love Him, you will become filled with a great desire
> To be like him . . . and do his will.
>
> As you draw nearer and nearer to Him . . .
> As your nature becomes more like His nature . . .
> He will draw nearer and nearer to you
> And the day will come when you shall know him.
>
> (June Andrew Babbel, *Onward and Upward* [Salt Lake City: Book-craft, Inc., 1980], p. 93.)

Believing the Promises

Let us examine two or three promises relating to our quest. The first was given by Jesus to his disciples as a standard that they should make known throughout their ministry. It reveals to us the key to the realization we seek.

> He that hath my commandments, and keepeth them, he it is that loveth me: and he that loveth me shall be loved of my Father, and I will love him, and will manifest myself to him. (John 14:21.)

The second promise was given by Jesus to us who are living in this day. In this promise he mentions five standards that we should meet.

> It shall come to pass that every soul who forsaketh his sins and cometh unto me, and calleth on my name, and obeyeth my voice,

and keepeth my commandments, shall see my face and know that I am. (D&C 93:1.)

You will observe in this promise that it applies to every soul. That includes all of us. Notice also the progression of these steps toward the goal. Ponder this promise and fulfill it. The promise will be honored in your behalf. Be patient. Remember always that the Lord is ready when you are.

Perhaps this is what the prophet Alma had in mind when he delivered his famous exhortation to his priesthood brethren:

> And now behold, I ask of you, my brethren of the church, have ye spiritually been born of God? Have ye received his image in your countenances? Have ye experienced this mighty change in your hearts? (Alma 5:14.)

Ask yourself these three questions. The answer to the first question about being spiritually born of God involves more than having hands laid upon your head for receipt of the Holy Ghost. It means fulfilling the first commandment you receive as a member of the Church to receive the Holy Ghost.

Receiving the right to the Holy Ghost is one thing. Taking that gift into your life and making it the forceful power that it ought to be is quite a different thing. Some never really achieve the status of being spiritually born of God. Yet this is a divine requirement for entrance into the kingdom of God.

The second question is "Have ye received his image in your countenance?" What is the image of Christ? Is it not one of Godly love? Is it not one of absolute purity? Is it not one of absolute honesty? Is it not one of absolute unselfishness? Do not these qualities bring forth a light that can be seen and felt?

When a person lives a genuine Christlike life, he will be able to fulfill the request of Jesus when he said, "Let your light so shine before men, that they may see your good works, and glorify your Father which is in heaven." (Matthew 5:16.)

And what about the third question, "Have ye experienced this mighty change in your hearts?"

Only you can answer this question honestly. This feeling of change cannot be mistaken. Does the feeling cause you to still pursue the course that the change brought about?

These are deeply searching questions, but they are very pertinent to our quest. In order to achieve a fulfillment of our desire, we must literally be holy as he is holy. Applying what we have considered so far and doing so in a genuine spirit of Christlike love, we most assuredly will not be disappointed, for God keeps his promises.

Consider well the following counsel and promise given by the Savior shortly before going with some of his chosen apostles to pray and agonize in the Garden of Gethsemane:

> I am the true vine, and my Father is the husbandman.
>
> Every branch in me that beareth not fruit he taketh away: and every branch that beareth fruit, he purgeth it, that it may bring forth more fruit.
>
> Abide in me, and I in you. As the branch cannot bear fruit of itself, except it abide in the vine; no more can ye, except ye abide in me.
>
> I am the vine, ye are the branches: He that abideth in me, and I in him, the same bringeth forth much fruit: for without me ye can do nothing.
>
> If ye abide in me, and my words abide in you, ye shall ask what ye will, and it shall be done unto you. (John 15:1-2, 4-5, 7.)

Experiencing the Second Comforter

Let us now take a searching look at this goal. Then we shall consider its implications. Elder B. H. Roberts, one of the Church's greatest historians, gives us this insight:

> . . . God is no respecter of persons . . . those who will approach him in faith . . . may have a knowledge of his existence . . . but . . . after any portion of the human family is made acquainted— either through tradition, or the testimony of those who have sought and found him—with the important fact that there is a God who has created and does uphold all things, the extent of their knowledge respecting his character and glory will depend upon their diligence and faithfulness in seeking after him: until, like Enoch, the brother of Jared, Moses, Joseph Smith, and Oliver Cowdery, they shall obtain faith in God, and power to behold him face to face. (*The Gospel and Man's Relationship to Deity*, first ed. [Salt Lake City: Contributor Co., 1888], p. 125.)

Although this pronouncement will require some deep pondering, it opens the opportunity for everyone who is inclined to behold our Lord face to face.

The Prophet Joseph Smith gave the first, and perhaps the best, explanation of what has come to be known as the Second Comforter. It is a thrilling concept and certainly a most challenging goal to attain.

> The other Comforter spoken of is a subject of great interest, and perhaps understood by few of this generation . . . Now what is this other Comforter? It is no more nor less than the Lord Jesus Christ Himself; and this is the sum and substance of the whole matter; that when any man obtains this last Comforter (the promise of eternal life), he will have the personage of Jesus Christ to attend him, or appear unto him from time to time, and even He will manifest the Father unto him, and they will take up their abode with him, and the visions of the heavens will be opened unto him, and the Lord will teach him face to face, and he may have a perfect knowledge of the mysteries of the Kingdom of God. (DHC 3:381.)

Those who receive the Second Comforter, or the promise of eternal life, have the privilege of communing personally and openly with God the Father and his son Jesus Christ. (D&C 107:18-19.) The Prophet Joseph Smith declared on several occasions that worthy Saints might enjoy the privilege of communing personally with both God the Father and his Son Jesus Christ. (D&C 130:3; Doctrine and Covenants Commentary, pp. 812-13.)

As we consider establishing such a divine attunement—and it will be at the option of the Savior, not us (unless we have faith like the Brother of Jared)—let us sense the thrill and wonder expressed by some of those who have experienced this union and made it a part of their history.

Here are testimonies of some persons in this dispensation who have recorded their privilege of seeing God the Father and/or Jesus Christ. For some of these a brief excerpt will suffice. Others will be presented in greater detail, since their description can help us visualize better what we are striving to become worthy to share. References to Joseph Smith, Oliver Cowdery, and Sidney Rigdon are not included since these are more readily available and are contained, in large part, in the Doctrine and Covenants and the history of the Church.

Newell Knight: A vision of futurity burst upon him. He saw . . . the heaven opened, and beheld the Lord Jesus Christ, seated at the right hand of the majesty on high and had it made plain to his understanding that the time would come when he would be admitted into His presence to enjoy His society for ever and ever. (*DHC* 1:85.)

Lyman Wight: He saw the heavens opened and the Son of Man sitting on the right hand of the Father, making intercession for his brethren. (*DHC* 1:176.)

Philo Dibble (commenting on Joseph Smith's and Sidney Rigdon's vision, D&C 76): I saw the glory and felt the power, but did not see the vision. (*Juvenile Instructor* 27:303.)

Alfred Douglas Young (September 17, 1841): Was constrained by the Spirit to go to some secret place. Out into the woods some distance from his brother's house, he was beckoned in vision by an angelic personage to "Follow thou me."

He ascended upward in the direction from whence he came and I followed him. He took me into the presence of God the Father and his Son, Jesus Christ. There was a rail between us; but I saw them seated on a throne. I had in my hands many sheaves of wheat of the purest white. There was an altar on my left hand and also one directly in front of me. The one on my left appeared to be about three feet in height, the one in front about eighteen inches. I laid the sheaves of wheat that were in my hands on the altar to my left as an offering to the Lord. I bowed myself on my knees on the altar in front of me, which was also in front of the throne.

I prayed God the Father in the name of his Son Jesus Christ to accept the offering I had laid upon the altar.

While I prayed the rail was removed and I stood upon my feet. Jesus arose and stepped from the side of his Father and came near where I stood. I was in their presence and I gazed upon their glory.

Jesus then said to me, "Your offering is accepted, and wouldst thou know the interpretation thereof?" I replied, "Yes, Lord." The angel, my conductor, said, "Look," and I saw as it were an innumerable company that had come up from all nations, kindreds, tongues, and peoples around the throne of God, and they fell down and worshipped Him and gave glory to Him. Jesus then said, "These are they thou shalt be the means of bringing into my Father's Kingdom and this is the interpretation of the offering thou hast laid upon the altar." (*Autobiographical Journal*, 1808-1842 [Historical Department, The Church of Jesus Christ of Latter-day Saints], pp. 3-13.)

Martin Harris (as recorded by Mary Elizabeth Rollins Lightner): They sang and prayed; then Joseph got up to speak. He began very solemnly and very earnestly. All at once his countenance changed and he stood mute. He turned so white he seemed perfectly transparent. Those who looked at him that night said he looked like he had a searchlight within him, in every part of his body. I never saw anything like it on earth. I could not take my eyes away from him. He got so white that anyone who saw him would have thought he was transparent. I remember I thought we could almost see the bones through the flesh of his face. I shall remember it and see it in my mind's eye as long as I remain upon the earth.

He stood some moments looking over the congregation, as if to pierce each heart, then said, "Do you know who has been in your midst this night?"

One of the Smiths said, "An angel of the Lord."

Joseph did not answer. Martin Harris was sitting at the Prophet's feet on a box. He slid to his knees, clasped his arms around the Prophet's knees and said, "I know, it was our Lord and Savior, Jesus Christ."

Joseph put his hand on Martin's head and answered, "Martin, God revealed that to you. Brothers and Sisters, the Savior has been in your midst this night. I want you all to remember it. There is a veil over your eyes, for you could not endure to look upon Him. You must be fed with milk and not strong meat. (Hyrum L. and Helen Mae Andrus, comp., *They Knew the Prophet* [Salt Lake City: Bookcraft, Inc., 1974], pp. 24-25.)

Alexander Neibaur, a Jewish convert from England: "Father (inquired his son), you have been telling us of your long and hard experience, and we have listened with intense affection and interest, but let me ask you, is it worth it all? Is the Gospel worth all this sacrifice?"

The glow of testimony and truth lighted the torches in the dimming eyes of that ancient Hebrew prophet and poet and he lifted his voice in firm and lofty assurance as he said:

"Yes! Yes! and more! I have seen my Savior. I have seen the prints in his hands! I know that Jesus is the Son of God, and I know that this work is true and that Joseph Smith was a prophet of God. I would suffer it all and more, far more than I have ever suffered for that knowledge even to the laying down of my body in the plains for the wolves to devour." (*The Utah Genealogical and Historical Magazine*, April 1914, 5:62.)

President George Q. Cannon (as was written and quoted at the time of his death): In faith, few were his equals. As a servant of the

Most High he was among the favored few who saw the face of the Lord while yet in the flesh and heard the Divine voice, and yet remained in mortality.

(At the October 1896 General Conference he gave this brief testimony): I know that God lives. I know that Jesus lives, for I have seen Him . . . I testify to you of these things as one that knows — as one of the Apostles of the Lord Jesus Christ that can bear witness to you today in the presence of the Lord Jesus Christ that he lives and that he will live and will come to reign on the earth, to sway an undisputed sceptre. (*Deseret Weekly*, April 1901, 53:610.)

President Lorenzo Snow (as related by his granddaughter, Allie Young Pond): One evening when I was visiting Grandpa Snow in his room in the Salt Lake Temple, I remained until the doorkeepers had gone and the night watchman had not yet come in, so grandpa said he would take me to the main front entrance and let me out that way. He got his bunch of keys from his dresser.

After we left his room and while we were still in the large corridor leading into the celestial room, I was walking several steps ahead of grandpa when he stopped me, saying, "Wait a moment, Allie. I want to tell you something. It was right here that the Lord Jesus Christ appeared to me at the time of the death of President Woodruff. He instructed me to go right ahead and reorganize the First Presidency of the Church at once and not wait as had been done after the death of the previous presidents, and that I was to succeed President Woodruff."

Then grandpa came a step nearer and held out his left hand and said: "He stood right here, about three feet from the floor. It looked as though He stood on a plate of solid gold."

Grandpa told me what a glorious personage the Savior is and described His hands, feet, countenance and beautiful White Robes, all of which were of such a glory of whiteness and brightness that he could hardly gaze upon Him.

Then grandpa came another step nearer me and put his right hand on my head and said: "Now, granddaughter, I want you to remember that this is the testimony of your grandfather, that he told you with his own lips that he actually saw the Savior here in the Temple and talked with Him face to face." (N. B. Lundwall, comp., *Temples of the Most High* [Salt Lake City: Bookcraft, Inc., n.d.], p. 141.)

Elder Orson F. Whitney: I seemed to be in the Garden of Gethsemane, a witness to the Savior's agony. I saw Him as plainly as ever I have seen anyone. Standing behind a tree in the foreground,

I beheld Jesus, with Peter, James and John, as they came through a little wicket gate at my right. Leaving the three Apostles there, after telling them to kneel and pray, the Son of God passed over to the other side, where He also knelt and prayed. It was the same prayer with which all Bible readers are familiar: "Oh my Father, if it be possible, let this cup pass from me; nevertheless not as I will, but as thou wilt."

As he prayed the tears streamed down his face, which was toward me. I was so moved at the sight that I also wept, out of pure sympathy. My whole heart went out to him; I loved him with all my soul, and longed to be with him as I longed for nothing else.

Presently He arose and walked to where those Apostles were kneeling—fast asleep! He shook them gently, awoke them, and in a tone of tender reproach, untinctured by the least show of anger or impatience, asked them plaintively if they could not watch with him one hour. There He was, with the awful weight of the world's sins upon his shoulders, with the pangs of every man, woman and child shooting through his sensitive soul—and they could not watch with him one poor hour!

Returning to his place, He offered up the same prayer as before; then went back and again found them sleeping. Again He awoke them, readmonished them, and once more returned and prayed. Three times this occurred, until I was perfectly familiar with his appearance—face, form and movements. He was of noble stature and majestic mien—not at all the weak, effeminate being that some painters have portrayed; but the very God that he was and is, as meek and humble as a little child.

All at once the circumstances seemed to change, the scene remaining just the same. Instead of before, it was after the crucifixion, and the Savior, with the three Apostles, now stood together in a group at my left. They were about to depart and ascent into Heaven. I could endure it no longer. I ran from behind the tree, fell at his feet, clasped Him around the knees, and begged him to take me with him.

I shall never forget the kind and gentle manner in which He stooped, raised me up, and embraced me. It was so vivid, so real, I felt the very warmth of his body, as He held me in his arms and said in tenderest tones: "No, my son, these have finished their work; they can go with me; but you must stay and finish yours." Still I clung to Him. Gazing into his face—for he was taller than I —I besought him fervently: "Well, promise me that I may come to you at the last." Smiling sweetly, He said, "That will depend entirely upon yourself." (Orson F. Whitney, *Through Memory's Halls* [Independence, Missouri: Zion's Printing and Publishing Co., 1930], p. 82.)

Elder Melvin J. Ballard: Away on the Fort Peck Reservation where I was doing missionary work with some of our brethren, laboring among the Indians, seeking the Lord for light to decide certain matters pertaining to our work there, and receiving a witness from Him that we were doing things according to His will, I found myself one evening in the dreams of the night in that sacred building, the temple. After a season of prayer and rejoicing I was informed that I should have the privilege of entering into one of those rooms, to meet a glorious Personage, and, as I entered the door, I saw, seated on a raised platform, the most glorious Being my eyes have ever beheld or that I ever conceived existed in all the eternal worlds. As I approached to be introduced, he arose and stepped towards me with extended arms, and he smiled as he softly spoke my name. If I shall live to be a million years old, I shall never forget that smile. He took me into his arms and kissed me, pressed me to his bosom, and blessed me, until the marrow of my bones seemed to melt! When he had finished, I fell at his feet, and, as I bathed them with my tears and kisses, I saw the prints of the nails in the feet of the Redeemer of the world. The feeling that I had in the presence of Him who hath all things in His hands, to have His love, His affection, and His blessing was such that if I ever can receive that which I had but a foretaste, I would give all that I am, all that I ever hope to be, to feel what I then felt! (*Melvin J. Ballard, Crusader for Righteousness* [Salt Lake City: Bookcraft, Inc., 1966], pp. 138-39.)

President David O. McKay: In the distance I beheld a beautiful white city. Though far away, yet I seemed to realize that trees with luscious fruit, shrubbery with gorgeously tinted leaves, and flowers in perfect bloom abounded everywhere. The clear sky above seemed to reflect these beautiful shades of color. I then saw a great concourse of people approaching the city. Each one wore a white flowing robe, and a white headdress. Instantly my attention seemed centered upon their Leader, and though I could see only the profile of his features and body, I recognized him at once as my Savior! The tint and radiance of his countenance were glorious to behold! There was a peace about him which seemed sublime—it was divine!

The city, I understood, was his. It was the City Eternal; and the people following him were to abide there in peace and eternal happiness.

But who were they?

As if the Savior read my thoughts, he answered by pointing to a semi-circle that then appeared above them, and on which were written in gold the words:

"These Are They Who Have Overcome The World—Who Have Truly Been Born Again!" (David O. McKay, *Cherished Experiences,* comp. Clare Middlemiss [Salt Lake City: Deseret Book Co., 1955], p. 102.)

President George F. Richards: It is not out of place for us to have important dreams . . . More than 40 years ago I had a dream which I am sure was from the Lord. In this dream I was in the presence of my Savior as He stood in mid-air. He spoke no word to me, but my love for him was such that I have not words to explain. I know no mortal man can love the Lord as I experienced that love for the Savior unless God reveals it to him. I would have remained in his presence, but there was a power drawing me away from him.

As a result of that dream, I had this feeling that no matter what might be required at my hands, what the gospel might entail unto me, I would do what I should be asked to do even to the laying down of my life . . .

If only I can be with my Savior and have that same sense of love that I had in that dream, it will be the goal of my existence, the desire of my life. (Spencer W. Kimball, "The Cause Is Just and Worthy," *Ensign,* May 1974, p. 119.)

In all of these cases, and in several unpublished ones with which I am personally familiar, this feeling of joy at experiencing this all-pervading glory and power of divine love cannot be described in words. It can only be experienced. All to whom this sacred privilege has been granted bear solemn witness that it is an experience for which no worthy effort is too great.

Before concluding this chapter and the message of this book, let us again remind ourselves of the following promises that will help us move toward these cherished goals that we have so far considered.

If a man love me, he will keep my words: and my Father will love him, and we will come unto him and make our abode with him! (John 14:23.)

The power and authority of the higher, or Melchizedek Priesthood, is to hold the keys of all the spiritual blessings of the church—

To have the privilege of receiving the mysteries of the kingdom of heaven, to have the heavens opened unto them, to commune with the general assembly and church of the Firstborn, and to enjoy the communion and presence of God the Father, and Jesus the Mediator of the new covenant. (D&C 107:18-19.)

So that we do not lose sight of our greater goal, B. H. Roberts helps us appreciate more fully what lies beyond this experience:

> That is the end, then for the spiritually born man—he will be conformed into the image of God—conformed to the type of the Spirit-life that has taken up his abode with him . . . The important thing for us . . . is that the spirit-birth takes place; that union with God be formed . . . The eternal years are his who is born of the Spirit; and again I say the important thing for us . . . is to have that Spirit-birth, and then are we sons of God; and while it doth not appear what we shall be, for the height and glory of that is beyond our human vision, ultimately we shall be like him, and see him as he is, and be conformed to the Christ image, that is to say, to the divine nature—unless one shall sin against the Holy Ghost. (B. H. Roberts, *Divine Immanence and the Holy Ghost* [Salt Lake City: Deseret News, 1912], p. 109.)

As a final indication of what such an achievement in our lives may hold in store for us, consider these promises from modern revelation:

> I, the Lord . . . delight to honor those who serve me in righteousness and in truth unto the end . . .
>
> And to them will I reveal all mysteries, yea, all the hidden mysteries of my kingdom from days of old, and for ages to come, will I make known unto them the good pleasure of my will concerning all things pertaining to my kingdom.
>
> Yea, even the wonders of eternity shall they know, and things to come will I show them, even the things of many generations.
>
> And their wisdom shall be great, and their understanding reach to heaven; and before them the wisdom of the wise shall perish, and the understanding of the prudent shall come to naught.
>
> For by my spirit will I enlighten them, and by my power will I make known unto them the secrets of my will—yea, even those things which eye has not seen, nor ear heard, nor yet entered into the heart of man.
>
> But great and marvelous are the works of the Lord, and the mysteries of his kingdom . . . which surpass all understanding in glory, and in might, and in dominion; . . .
>
> Which . . . are not lawful for man to utter;
>
> Neither is man capable to make them known, for they are only

to be seen and understood by the power of the Holy Spirit, which God bestows on those who love him, and purify themselves before him;

. . . to whom he grants this privilege of seeing and knowing for themselves;

That through the power and manifestation of the Spirit, while in the flesh, they may be able to bear his presence in the world of glory. (D&C 76:5, 7-10, 114-118.)

May each person who reads, ponders, and earnestly applies the truths presented in this book catch the spirit of being the maker of his or her own destiny, ever remembering that Jesus Christ is the author and finisher of our faith.

Working in partnership with the Lord, may each of us gladly and reverently respond to his challenge.

Therefore, what manner of men [and women] ought ye to be? Verily I say unto you, even as I am! (3 Nephi 27:27.)

May we then each have this divine promise increasingly fulfilled in our own lives:

And this is life eternal, that they might know thee the only true God, and Jesus Christ, whom thou hast sent. (John 17:3.)

Index